ReviseIB

IB Diploma Programme
BIOLOGY
Exam Practice Workbook

Second Edition

A note from us

While every effort has been made to provide accurate advice on the assessments for this subject, the only authoritative and definitive source of guidance and information is published in the official subject guide, teacher support materials, specimen papers and associated content published by the IB. Please refer to these documents in the first instance for advice and guidance on your assessments.

Any exam-style questions in this book have been written to help you practise and revise your knowledge and understanding of the content before your exam. Remember that the actual exam questions may not look like this.

Sarah Bragg

Nadia Jaradat

SL

Published by Extend Education Ltd., Sunningend Business Centre, Unit 22 Lansdown Industrial Estate, Cheltenham, UK, GL51 8PL

www.extendeducation.com

The right of Sarah Bragg and Nadia Jaradat to be identified as the authors of this work has been asserted by them with the Copyright, Designs and Patents Act 1988.

Typesetting by York Publishing Solutions Pvt. Ltd., INDIA

First published 2022

This edition first published 2025.

25 24 23 22 21

10 9 8 7 6 5 4 3 2 1

ISBN 978-1-913121-85-3

Copyright notice

All rights reserved. No part of this publication may be reproduced, stored in a retrieval system or transmitted in any form or by any means, electronic, mechanical, photocopying, recording or otherwise, without permission in writing from the copyright owner, except in accordance with the provisions of the Copyright, Designs and Patents Act 1988 or under the terms of a licence from the Copyright Licensing Agency Limited. Further details of such licences (for reprographic reproduction) may be obtained from the Copyright Licensing Agency Limited, Barnard's Inn, 86 Fetter Lane, London EC4A 1EN (www.cla.co.uk). Applications for the copyright owner's written permission should be addressed to the publisher.

Other important information

A reminder that Extend Education is not in any way affiliated with the International Baccalaureate.

Many people have worked to create this book. We go through rigorous editorial processes, including separate answers checks and expert reviews of all content. However, we all make mistakes. So if you notice an error in the book, please let us know at info@extendeducation.co.uk so we can make sure it is corrected at the earliest possible opportunity.

If you are an educator with a passion for creating content and would like to write for us, please contact info@extendeducation.co.uk or write to us through the contact form on our website www.extendeducation.co.uk.

Permissions

Daniele Pugliesi (CC BY-SA 3.0), p.11; Louisa Howard, p.13; Jerry Crimson Mann (CC BY-SA 3.0), p.18; Yuv345 (CC BY-SA 4.0), p24; Rosser1954 (CC BY-SA 4.0), p.28; albert kok (CC BY-SA 3.0), p.40; Alan Wilson (CC BY-SA 3.0), p.42; J. Patrick Fischer (CC BY-SA 3.0) p.42; Jean Beaufort, p.42; David Iliff (CC BY-SA 3.0), p.42; Chris Heaton / Bluebells in Bigsweir Wood (CC BY-SA 2.0), p.45; Beatriz Moisset (CC BY-SA 4.0), p.46; Carny (CC BY 2.5), p.50; Quasar Jarosz (CC BY-SA 3.0), p.67; Spiga, p.68; Cancer Research UK / Wikimedia Commons (CC BY-SA 4.0), p.69; Isometrik (CC BY-SA 3.0), p.70; US Geological Survey (USGS), p.71; Doc. RNDr. Josef Reischig, CSc (CC BY-SA 3.0), p.74; Jon Houseman (CC BY-SA 4.0), p.82.

Every effort has been made to locate and contact copyright holders of material reproduced in this book. If notified, the publishers will be pleased to rectify any errors or omissions at the earliest opportunity.

CONTENTS

HOW TO USE THIS BOOK	4
YOUR PAPERS	5

SET A

Paper 1A	7
Paper 1B	20
Paper 2	24

SET B

Paper 1A	34
Paper 1B	46
Paper 2	51

SET C

Paper 1A	60
Paper 1B	72
Paper 2	77

ANSWERS

Set A:	Paper 1A	86
	Paper 1B	86
	Paper 2	86
Set B:	Paper 1A	88
	Paper 1B	88
	Paper 2	88
Set C:	Paper 1A	90
	Paper 1B	90
	Paper 2	90

HOW TO USE THIS BOOK

This exam practice book helps you prepare for your DP Biology Standard Level exam. It is divided into three sets of papers.

Paper 1A, Paper 1B and Paper 2

Presented with a lot of tips and guidance to help you to get to the correct answer and boost your confidence!

Use these papers early on in your revision.

Set B

Paper 1A, Paper 1B and Paper 2

Presented with fewer helpful suggestions so you have to rely on your revision when trying these.

Test yourself using these papers when you are a bit more confident.

Paper 1A, Paper 1B and Paper 2

Presented with space to add your own notes and no guidance – the perfect way to test whether you are exam ready.

Use these papers as close as you can to the exam.

The first set of papers has a lot of helpful tips and suggestions for answering the questions. The middle set has more general advice – make sure you have revised before testing yourself with this set. The last set has no help at all. Not one single hint! Make sure you do this one a bit closer to your exam to check what else you might need to revise.

Features

Take a look at some of the helpful features in these books that are designed to support you as you do your practice papers.

These will point you in the direction of the right answer!

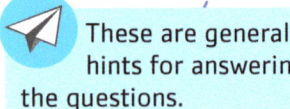

These are general hints for answering the questions.

These are referred to as AOs all the way through this book

This box reminds you of the assessment objective being tested.

Beware of making common and easy-to-avoid mistakes!

! These flag up common or easy-to-make mistakes that might cost you marks.

The command terms are like a clue to how you should answer your questions

COMMAND TERMS

These boxes outline what the command term is asking you to do.

Link to TOK

These show you when the questions have other interdisciplinary links.

These boxes contain really useful advice about what examiners are looking for

ANSWER ANALYSIS

These boxes help you to think about the answer you are giving in more detail or include advice on how to get the highest possible marks for your answer.

Answers

Answers to all questions are included at the back of the book so you can check how you did.

Find the answers on page 86!

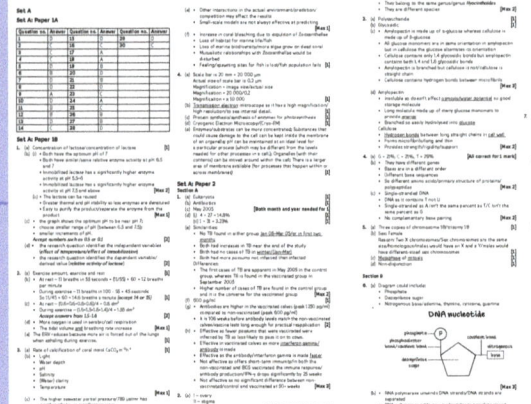

YOUR PAPERS

Knowing the requirements of your exam papers is as important as your knowledge about the topic. The structure of the paper shouldn't be a surprise to you during the exam session.

How are you assessed?

You will sit two written papers for your exams.

Paper 1		Paper 2	
Paper 1A	Paper 1B	Section A	Section B
30 multiple-choice questions	Data-based questions (four questions that are syllabus related, addressing all themes)	Data-based questions. Short answer questions	Extended-response questions 1 of 2 extended-response questions to be answered.
30 marks	25 marks	34 marks	16 marks
36% of final grade		44% of final grade	
1 hour 30 minutes		1 hour 30 minutes	

> Try to keep your writing inside the boxes as these are what the examiner scans when they are marking. If you go outside the box, write 'continued on lined paper' at the bottom. Then, label the lined extra paper with the question number clearly.

Assessment objectives

There are **three** assessment objectives for your DP Biology exams. Make sure you are clear on what you are expected to demonstrate for each one.

Assessment objective	Command terms	Which questions test this?	Example question
Assessment objective 1: Demonstrate knowledge of: • terminology, facts and concepts • skills, techniques and methodologies.	Define Draw Label List Measure State	Questions in the exam that test your understanding of AO1 are asking you to demonstrate knowledge and comprehension of different aspects of biology: • key terms and biological concepts • biological methodologies and techniques • how to communicate scientific information.	State which domain the infected cows belong to. [1] List **two** characteristics of stem cells. [2] Define invasive species. [1]
Assessment objective 2: Understand and apply knowledge of: • terminology and concepts • skills, techniques and methodologies.	Annotate Calculate Describe Distinguish Estimate Identify Outline	Questions in the exam that test your understanding of AO2 are generally asking you to apply and analyse your knowledge. You may also be asked to use examples of biological methodologies and techniques, as well as how to communicate scientific knowledge, when answering a specific question.	Calculate the magnification of the image. [1] Use information from the text above to identify a treatment for humans who have contracted Bovine tuberculosis. [1]

Assessment objective	Command terms	Which questions test this?	Example question
Assessment objective 3: Analyse, evaluate, and synthesize: • experimental procedures • primary and secondary data • trends, patterns and predictions.	Analyse Comment Compare Compare and contrast Construct Deduce Design Determine Discuss Evaluate Explain Justify Predict Sketch Suggest	Questions in the exam that test your understanding of AO3 are asking you to evaluate research questions and predictions. You will be asked to formulate and analyse primary and secondary data with explanations, using scientific methodologies and techniques.	Based on the graph, compare and contrast the infection rates with TB in the control and vaccinated groups. [2] Using all the data, evaluate the use of vaccination to prevent the spread of TB to domestic livestock. [3] Explain the control of the cell cycle. [3]

Command terms

Assessment objective 1

Command term	Definition
Define	Give the precise meaning of a word, phrase, concept or physical quantity.
Draw	Represent by means of a labelled, accurate diagram or graph, using a pencil. A ruler (straight edge) should be used for straight lines. Diagrams should be drawn to scale. Graphs should have points correctly plotted (if appropriate) and joined in a straight line or smooth curve.
Label	Add labels to a diagram.
List	Give a sequence of brief answers with no explanation.
Measure	Obtain a value for a quantity.
State	Give a specific name, value or other brief answer without explanation or calculation.

Assessment objective 2

Command term	Definition
Annotate	Add brief notes to a diagram or graph.
Calculate	Obtain a numerical answer showing the relevant stages in the working.
Describe	Give a detailed account.
Distinguish	Make clear the differences between two or more concepts or items.
Estimate	Obtain an approximate value.
Identify	Provide an answer from a number of possibilities.
Outline	Give a brief account or summary.

Assessment objective 3

Command term	Definition
Analyse	Break down in order to bring out the essential elements or structure.
Comment	Give a judgement based on a given statement or result of a calculation. Appendices
Compare	Give an account of the similarities between two (or more) items or situations, referring to both (all) of them throughout.
Compare and contrast	Give an account of similarities and differences between two (or more) items or situations, referring to both (all) of them throughout.
Construct	Display information in a diagrammatic or logical form.
Deduce	Reach a conclusion from the information given.
Design	Produce a plan, simulation or model.
Determine	Obtain the only possible answer.
Discuss	Offer a considered and balanced review that includes a range of arguments, factors or hypotheses. Opinions or conclusions should be presented clearly and supported by appropriate evidence.
Evaluate	Make an appraisal by weighing up the strengths and limitations.
Explain	Give a detailed account including reasons or causes.
Justify	Give valid reasons or evidence to support an answer or conclusion.
Predict	Give an expected result.
Sketch	Represent by means of a diagram or graph (labelled as appropriate). The sketch should give a general idea of the required shape or relationship, and should include relevant features.
Suggest	Propose a solution, hypothesis or other possible answer.

EXAM PRACTICE

In this section, you can test yourself with different sets of practice papers under exam conditions.

All you need is this book, a timer, a pen and some extra paper to use if you run out of answer lines. Then you can check your answers at the back of the book when you're done.

You might want to take at least a day's break between Paper 1A/B and Paper 2.

Set A

Paper 1A: Standard Level

Set your timer for 1 hour 30 minutes **[Paper 1A and Paper 1B]**.

- Each question is worth **[1]** mark.
- For each question, choose the answer you consider to be the best and put a tick next to it in the book.
- A calculator is required for this paper.
- The maximum mark for paper 1A is **[30 marks]**.

1. Which of the following properties of water explains the transport of heat through the blood from the liver? **[1]**
   - ☐ A. Universal solvent
   - ☐ B. High latent heat of vaporization
   - ☐ C. Adhesion
   - ☐ D. High specific heat capacity

2. If 30% of DNA is cytosine, how much is adenine? **[1]**
   - ☐ A. 70%
   - ☐ B. 50%
   - ☐ C. 20%
   - ☐ D. 10%

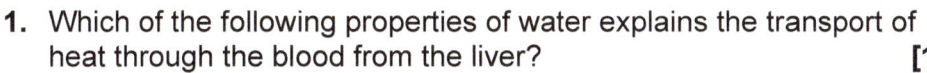

 Remember that **(A+T) + (C+G) = 100%** because DNA is double stranded.

> 🔍 **ANSWER ANALYSIS**
>
> The papers in Set A have a lot of additional tips in the margin to help you get to the right answer. If you need to look at the answer key at the back, or give yourself more time, go ahead – you are just practising how to do the paper.

> ❗ In the real exam, you will be writing your answers on a separate answer sheet provided.

> ❗ Make sure you do not get confused between 'adhesion' and 'cohesion'.

> ❗ **High latent heat of vaporization** refers to the evaporation of water whereas **high specific heat capacity** refers to the large amount of energy needed to increase the temperature.

> 🔍 **ANSWER ANALYSIS**
>
> If there is 30% cytosine in the DNA then how much must be guanine? Think of complementary base pairing (C+G). The remaining DNA is the percentage for both adenine and thymine (A+T). How would you find adenine only?

3. Below is a diagram of a DNA nucleotide. [1]

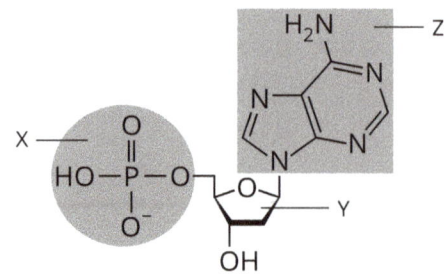

Identify X, Y and Z.

	X	Y	Z
☐ A.	Nitrogenous base	Ribose sugar	Phosphate
☐ B.	Phosphate	Ribose sugar	Nitrogenous base
☐ C.	Phosphate	Deoxyribose sugar	Nitrogenous base
☐ D.	Nitrogenous base	Ribose sugar	Ribose sugar

4. Which molecule found in plants has 1,4 glycosidic bonds and 1,6 glycosidic bonds? [1]

☐ A. Glycogen

☐ B. Amylose

☐ C. Amylopectin

☐ D. Polypeptide

5. Which of the molecules below corresponds to the correct name? [1]

	Molecule	Name
☐ A.	(cyclic sugar structure with CH₂OH)	Unsaturated fatty acid
☐ B.	(dipeptide structure)	β-glucose
☐ C.	(long saturated hydrocarbon chain with COOH)	Amino acid
☐ D.	(four-ringed steroid structure)	Steroid

 This is a nucleotide with the shapes that match the circle, pentagon and rectangle in the syllabus. It is just shown in more detail.

 Polypeptides contain peptide bonds.

Glycogen is a branching polysaccharide which contains both 1,4 glycosidic bonds and 1,6 glycosidic bonds. It is found in muscle cells and the liver of animals.

Amylose is found in plants but only contains 1,4 glycosidic bonds.

Amylopectin is a branching plant storage compound made up of alpha-glucose monomers joined by condensation reactions.

 Fatty acids have a methyl end (CH_3), a long hydrocarbon chain and a carboxylic acid (carboxyl) end (COOH). **Saturated fats** have the general formula ($CH_3(CH_2)$ COOH) as every carbon bond in the chain is bonded to two hydrogen atoms. **Unsaturated fats** still have the methyl and carboxylic acid groups, but the hydrocarbon chain contains a carbon to carbon double bond (C=C). Fatty acids contain very little oxygen.

 Steroids contain four linked rings.

 Sugars contain carbon rings with lots of OH bonds allowing them to be soluble in water.

 All amino acids contain an amine group (NH_2) at one end and carboxylic acid group (COOH) at the other. The central carbon is bonded to an H and an R group. The simplest R group is an H found in glycine.

6. Which is the correct protein and description? [1]

	I	II
☐ A.	Alpha Amylase	Transports oxygen in red blood cells
☐ B.	Insulin	Hormone responsible for regulation blood glucose levels
☐ C.	Collagen	Enzyme that digests bacteria cell walls
☐ D.	Haemoglobin	Strong structural protein in ligaments and skin

The protein **alpha amylase** has one polypeptide and is produced by the salivary glands and pancreas. It digests starch into maltose molecules.

The protein **insulin** is made up of two polypeptide chains. It is responsible for controlling blood sugar levels.

The protein **collagen** has a high tensile strength.

Haemoglobin in erythrocytes binds to oxygen in the lungs where there is a high concentration of oxygen. It releases the oxygen in the muscles where there is a low concentration of oxygen.

7. The effect of temperature on an enzyme-controlled reaction is investigated in an experiment. What could the dependent variable be? [1]

☐ A. Changing the temperature

☐ B. Keeping the mass of enzyme the same

☐ C. Changing the concentration of the substrate

☐ D. Measuring the rate of the product formed

Make sure you know the difference between the independent variable (what you change), the dependent variable (what you measure) and the controlled variables (what you keep the same so the experiment is valid/a fair test).

8. Yeast cells *Saccharomyces cerevisiae* were incubated with four different carbohydrates and a control with no carbohydrate for 10 minutes. The volume of carbon dioxide released from anaerobic respiration (fermentation) was measured with a gas syringe. This graph shows the results.

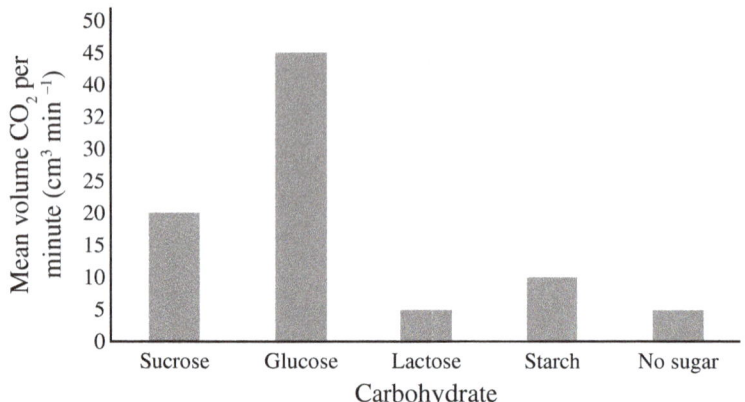

What conclusion can be drawn from the results of this experiment? [1]

☐ A. Yeast cannot use polysaccharides for respiration

☐ B. Lactose can be used in respiration

☐ C. More glucose is made than any other sugar

☐ D. Sucrose increases respiration rates more than starch

> Polysaccharides contain many monosaccharides joined by glycosidic bonds; they include starch (amylose and amylopectin), cellulose and glycogen.

> Disaccharides contain two monosaccharides joined together by a glycosidic bond. For example, sucrose is made up of the monosaccharides glucose and fructose. Lactose is made up of glucose and galactose.

> A control of 'no sugar' is used as a comparison to see if the yeast respired using the sugar in its cytoplasm.

9. This graph shows the absorbance of light for chlorophyll a and b:

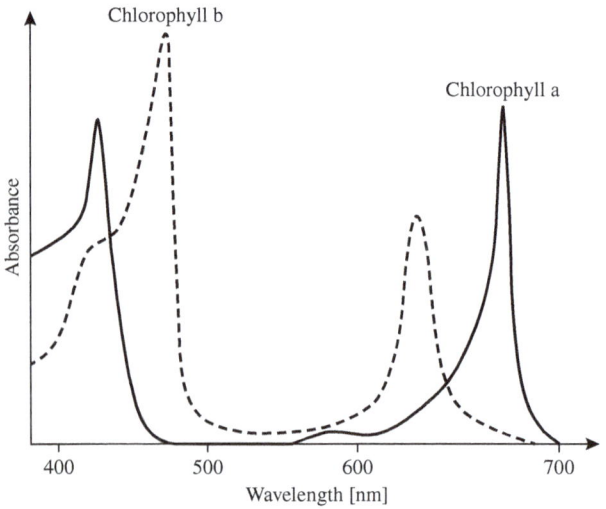

What conclusions can be drawn from the graph? [1]

☐ A. Chlorophyll a is more efficient at absorbing red light than chlorophyll b

☐ B. Chlorophyll a is more efficient at absorbing blue light than chlorophyll b

☐ C. Chlorophyll a and b are efficient at absorbing green light

☐ D. There is more chlorophyll b pigment than chlorophyll a in leaves

> In the electromagnetic spectrum for visible light:
> - red has the longest wavelength at approximately 700 nm
> - green is shorter at approximately 500 nm
> - blue is the shortest wavelength at approximately 450 nm.
>
> Look at each statement for the wavelengths stated.

> If we see a green object, it absorbs other colours and reflects green into our eyes.

10. How can fragments of DNA be separated? [1]
   - ☐ A. Using somatic gene transfer
   - ☐ B. Using polymerase chain reaction (PCR)
   - ☐ C. Using cloning
   - ☐ D. Using gel electrophoresis

 Cloning is the generation of genetically identical cells or organisms.

11. Which sequence of bases and amino acids could be made by the transcription and translation of the DNA molecule shown? [1]

   3' ATGGAATATCGATTTAAA 5'
   5' TACCTTATAGCTAAATTT 3'

		2nd base in codon				
		U	C	A	G	
		Phe	Ser	Tyr	Cys	U
	U	Phe	Ser	Tyr	Cys	C
		Leu	Ser	Stop	Stop	A
		Leu	Ser	Stop	Trp	G
		Leu	Pro	His	Arg	U
1st base in codon	C	Leu	Pro	His	Arg	C
		Leu	Pro	Gln	Arg	A
		Leu	Pro	Gln	Arg	G
		Ile	Thr	Asn	Ser	U
	A	Ile	Thr	Asn	Ser	C
		Ile	Thr	Lys	Arg	A
		Ile	Thr	Lys	Arg	G
		Val	Ala	Asp	Gly	U
	G	Val	Ala	Asp	Gly	C
		Val	Ala	Glu	Gly	A
		Val	Ala	Glu	Gly	G

(3rd base in codon)

	Sequence of bases	Sequence of amino acids
☐ A.	UAC-AUA-AAA-UUU-CUU-GCU	Tyr-Ile-Lys-Phe-Leu-Ala
☐ B.	UAC-CUU-AUA-GCU-AAA-UUU	Tyr-Leu-Ile-Ala-Lys-Phe
☐ C.	UAU-AUC-GAA-CGA-UUU-AAA	Tyr-Ile-Glu-Arg-Phe-Lys
☐ D.	UAU-GAA-CGA-UUU-AAA	Tyr-Glu-Arg-Phe-Lys

Somatic gene transfer involves placing a healthy human gene into a living person's body who has a faulty copy of the (somatic) cells. This means the recipient can then express the transferred gene.

DNA is amplified using a polymerase chain reaction. It is then chopped into fragments using restriction enzymes. The fragments are put into an electrophoresis chamber where the negatively charged DNA moves towards the positive electrode. Small fragments travel further from the origin than large fragments.

 ANSWER ANALYSIS

The table uses mRNA codons so you need to work out the mRNA sequence.

The DNA code containing the genetic information is on the **sense strand**, which is read in the 5' to 3' direction. The **antisense strand** is used as the template to make the mRNA. The mRNA will read the same as the DNA 5' to 3' but with a U instead of T.
mRNA = UACCUUAUAGCUAAAUUU

 ANSWER ANALYSIS

- Look up UAC in the table: U = First row, A = third column, C = second line.
- Read the amino acid name in the first row, third column, second line = Tyr.
- Repeat with the rest of the codons.

12. Why are aseptate fungi considered atypical eukaryotic cells? [1]
    - ☐ A. They are made from pre-existing cells by mitosis
    - ☐ B. They consist of multinucleated hypha
    - ☐ C. They only have one nucleus but it is very large
    - ☐ D. They lack a cell wall

13. The following electron micrograph shows part of a lung cell.

    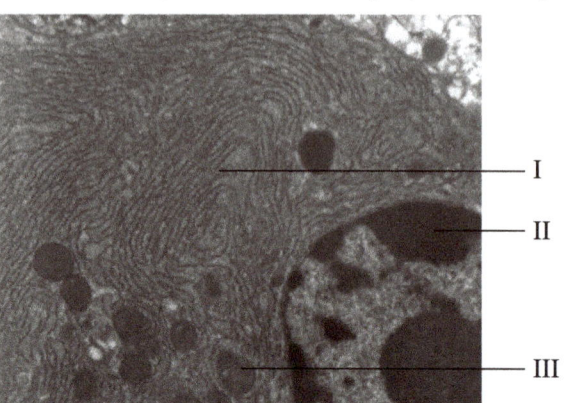

    Which organelles correspond to the labels in the electron micrograph of this cell? [1]

	I	II	III
☐ A.	Golgi apparatus	Nucleus	Chloroplast
☐ B.	Rough endoplasmic reticulum	Nucleoid	Mitochondria
☐ C.	Golgi apparatus	Nucleoid	Chloroplast
☐ D.	Rough endoplasmic reticulum	Nucleus	Mitochondria

14. Surface area to volume ratio is important in limiting cell size. Which statement about factors that limit cell size is true? [1]
    - ☐ A. A larger cell has a lower rate of metabolism and a larger surface area than a small cell
    - ☐ B. A larger cell has a lower rate of metabolism and a smaller surface area than a small cell
    - ☐ C. A larger cell has a higher rate of metabolism and a smaller surface area to volume ratio than a small cell
    - ☐ D. A larger cell has a lower rate of metabolism and a larger surface area than a small cell

15. Sweet potato (*Ipomoea batatas*) and potato (*Solanum tuberosum*) cubes were placed in different strength salt solutions varying from 0.0 mol dm^{-3} to 1.0 mol dm^{-3} for 1 hour. The percentage change in mass of each tissue was calculated and plotted on the graph below.

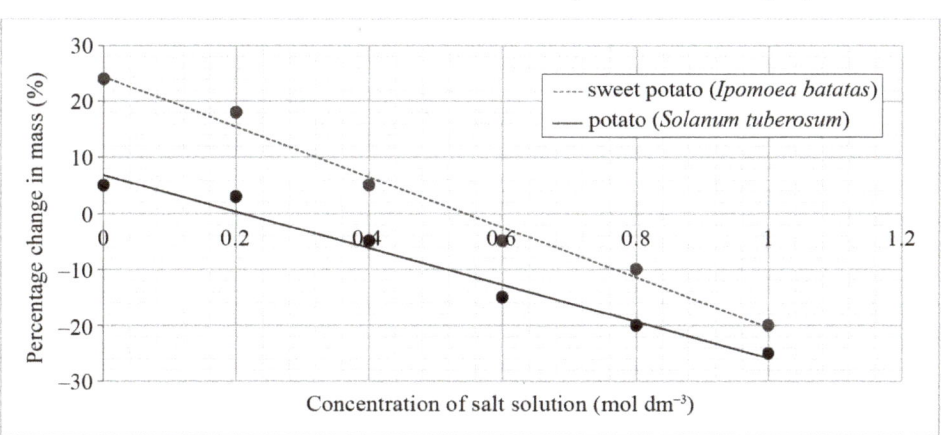

Use the graph to deduce which statement is correct. [1]

- A. At 0.4 mol dm^{-3} the potato is in a hypertonic solution, but the sweet potato is in a hypotonic solution
- B. At 0.2 mol dm^{-3} the solution is isotonic with the sweet potato
- C. The sweet potato has a lower concentration of solutes in its cytoplasm than potato
- D. Below 0.2 mol dm^{-3} both tissues are in hypertonic solutions

Osmosis is the movement of water from a hypotonic (dilute) solution to a hypertonic (concentrated) solution across a partially permeable membrane.

If water **enters** a cell, the cell will **gain** mass. If water **leaves** a cell, the cell will **lose** mass. If the cell does not gain or lose mass, it has the **same concentration** as the solution (isotonic).

Water evaporates from leaves through a gap called a stoma – no membrane is involved. **Sweat** freely evaporates from the surface of the skin.

16. How does the sodium-potassium pump contribute to membrane potential? [1]

- A. It pumps more sodium ions into the cell than potassium ions out, creating a positive interior.
- B. It pumps sodium and potassium ions equally, leading to no change in charge distribution.
- C. It moves three sodium ions out and two potassium ions in, making the inside of the cell more negative.
- D. It allows sodium and potassium to move freely across the membrane, eliminating membrane potential.

The sodium-potassium pump is an active transport mechanism that moves ions against their concentration gradients using ATP.

For every three sodium ions (Na$^+$) pumped out, only two potassium ions (K$^+$) are pumped in.

This imbalance creates a net loss of positive charge inside the cell, helping to maintain a negative resting membrane potential.

17. The image shows chromosomes in meiosis. What stage of meiosis are they in? [1]

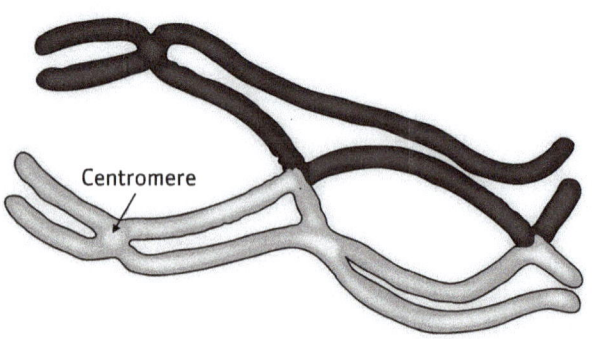

- A. Prophase I
- B. Prophase II
- C. Anaphase I
- D. Anaphase II

> The overlaps where homologous chromosomes cross over are called chiasmata and are a source of variation in gametes. This crossing over occurs in prophase I of meiosis between non-sister chromatids.

18. What does the karyogram below correspond to? [1]

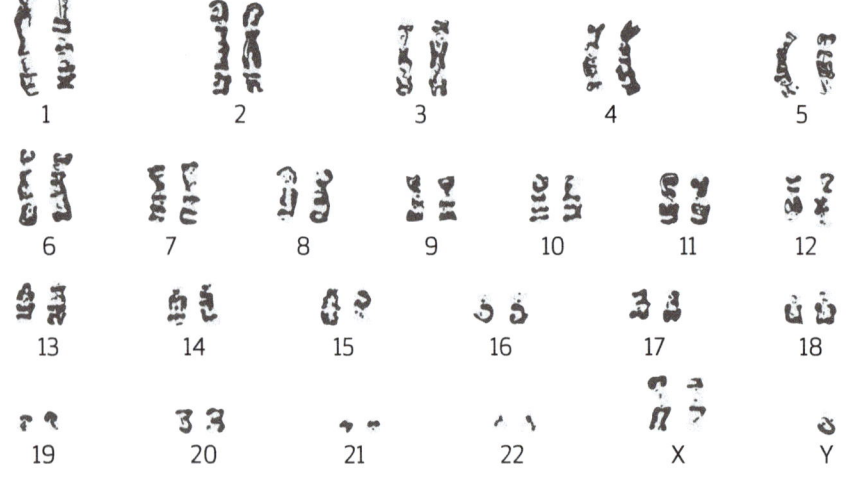

- A. Non-disjunction of sex chromosomes (Klinefelter syndrome)
- B. Normal female
- C. Female with Down syndrome
- D. Normal male

> XX = female
> XY = male
> Non-disjunction occurs when either homologous chromosomes fail to split before migrating to poles in anaphase I or when sister chromatids fail to split before migrating to poles in anaphase II. As a result, the gamete has an extra chromosome. After fertilization, the zygote will have 2 copies from this gamete and another from the pairing gamete so it will have three copies of the chromosome.

19. A mouse has the diploid number of 40 chromosomes. How many autosomes are in a mouse sperm cell? [1]

- A. 20
- B. 19
- C. 40
- D. 38

> Autosomes are any chromosomes that do not determine the sex of the mouse. There are 38 autosomes (non-sex cells) and 2 sex cells (X and Y) out of the 40.

> The diploid number of chromosomes in a mouse is 40 (or 20 pairs). When gametes are made only one of each chromosome pair will pass into the gamete.

> The sperm cell will have the haploid number of 20 chromosomes. One of which will be a sex cell so that leaves 19 autosomes.

20. Which of the following methods can archaea not use to provide the energy for ATP production? [1]

   ☐ A. Light energy
   ☐ B. Oxidation of inorganic chemicals
   ☐ C. Oxidation of carbon compounds
   ☐ D. Heat energy

21. What characteristics do embryonic stem cells show? [1]

   ☐ A. Multipotent and totiopotent
   ☐ B. Totiopotent and pluripotent
   ☐ C. Only pluripotent
   ☐ D. Only multipotent

22. Which structure is shown in the following image? [1]

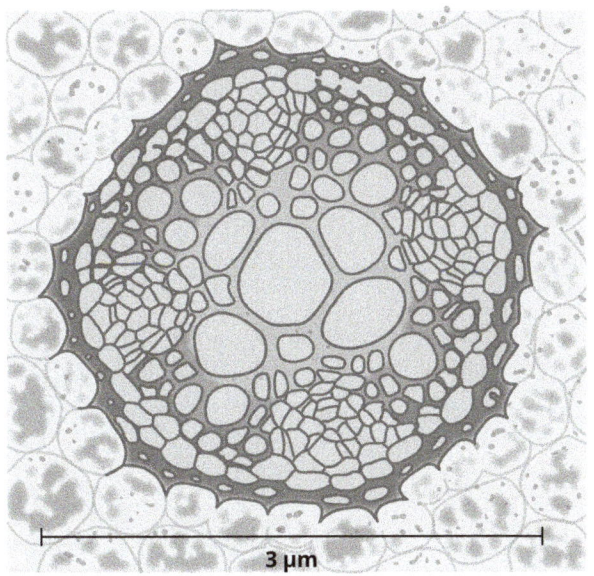

   ☐ A. Cross-section of a leaf
   ☐ B. Cross-section of a dicotyledon stem
   ☐ C. Cross-section of a flower
   ☐ D. Cross-section of a dicotyledon root

23. Jet lag results during travel due to disruption of circadian rhythms. The lack of which hormone can cause jet lag? **[1]**

- ☐ A. Leptin
- ☐ B. Epinephrine
- ☐ C. Melatonin
- ☐ D. Insulin

> **Insulin** lowers blood sugar and is made in the beta cells of the islets of Langerhans in the pancreas.
> **Epinephrine** (also called adrenaline) is made by the adrenal glands to prepare the body for its 'flight or fight' response.
> **Leptin** is released by adipose (fat) cells to inhibit hunger.
> **Melatonin** is important in the regulation of the circadian rhythms and sleep.

24. What is the correct sequence of blood clotting? **[1]**

- ☐ A. Thrombin – fibrinogen – fibrin
- ☐ B. Fibrinogen – fibrin – thrombin
- ☐ C. Fibrin – fibrinogen – thrombin
- ☐ D. Thrombin – fibrin – fibrinogen

> The cascade of reactions occurring as a result of the release of clotting factors allows for the formation of thrombin. Thrombin then catalyses the conversion of the soluble globular protein fibrinogen into the insoluble protein fibrin. Fibrin than traps red blood cells and platelets. This forms a scab that acts as a barrier to pathogens.

> Clotting factors released by the damaged cell cause platelets to plug the damaged area.

25. What is the correct sequence for the germination of a broad bean (*Vicia faba*) seed? **[1]**

☐ A.	Imbibes water	Gibberellin produced	Amylase breaks down starch to maltose	Plumule emerges followed by radicle
☐ B.	Gibberellin produced	Imbibes water	Amylase breaks down starch to maltose	Radicle emerges followed by plumule
☐ C.	Imbibes water	Gibberellin produced	Amylase breaks down starch to maltose	Radicle emerges followed by plumule
☐ D.	Gibberellin produced	Imbibes water	Amylase breaks down starch to maltose	Plumule emerges followed by radicle

> A seed needs oxygen, water and warmth to germinate. In these conditions it will absorb water through the micropyle. This rehydrates the tissue allowing the embryo to make the hormone gibberellin. The seed then produces the enzyme amylase which breaks starch to maltose. Maltose is then broken down to glucose for respiration or used to make cellulose for the cell wall. Energy from respiration is used to build tissue that grows into a radicle (small root) and then a plumule (small shoot) followed by photosynthetic leaves.

26. The diagram shows a pedigree of polydactyly, a disease in which an affected person has an extra finger. Individuals with the disorder are shown as shaded.

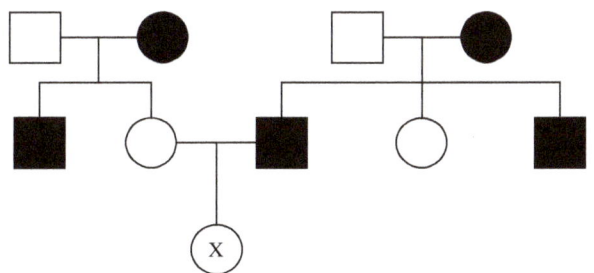

What is the chance that the individual labelled X has the disorder? **[1]**

- ☐ A. 100%
- ☐ B. 50%
- ☐ C. 25%
- ☐ D. 0%

> Recessive traits will have some unaffected parents having affected children. It is not possible for two affected parents (homozygous recessive) to have an unaffected child. **Dominant** traits will have a parent affected in every generation. It is possible for two affected parents to have an unaffected child if both parents are heterozygous.

ANSWER ANALYSIS

> You can work out that polydactyly is an **X-linked recessive** trait.

> The father of individual x has the disorder. So she must inherit one affected X chromosome from him.
> Her mother must be a carrier because her grandmother had the disorder.

27. Which statement about evolution is correct? **[1]**

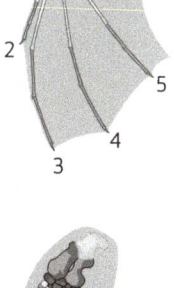

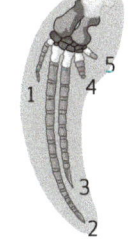

- ☐ A. The bat wing and dolphin flipper are homologous in structure, giving evidence for convergent evolution
- ☐ B. The bat wing and dolphin flipper are homologous in structure, giving evidence for divergent evolution
- ☐ C. The bat wing and dolphin flipper are analogous in structure, giving evidence for convergent evolution
- ☐ D. The bat wing and dolphin flipper are analogous in structure, giving evidence for divergent evolution

> Homologous evolution refers to similar structures that have adapted over time to develop different functions (adaptive radiation) as a result of natural selection. This similarity in structure suggests the organisms have a common ancestor.

> Analogous structures are not similar in their structure but do have a similar function.

28. A food chain is shown below. Which creatures are the primary consumer? [1]

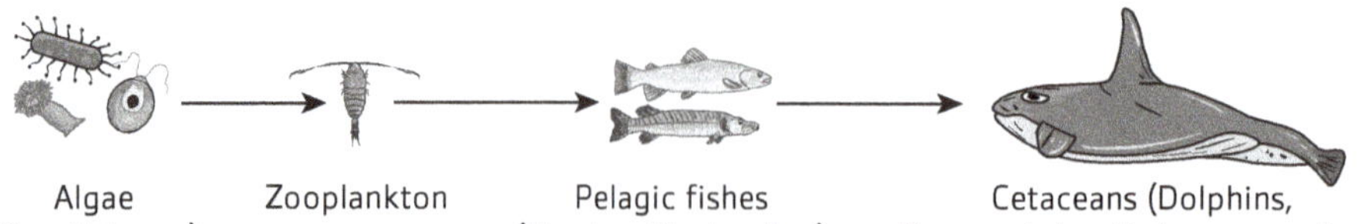

Algae (flagellates, ...) → Zooplankton → Pelagic fishes (Herring, Mackerel, ...) → Cetaceans (Dolphins, Sperm whales, Harbour porpoises)

- ☐ A. Algae
- ☐ B. Zooplankton
- ☐ C. Pelagic fishes
- ☐ D. Cetaceans

> A producer will always be the first trophic level. It is an organism that can produce food from inorganic compounds and is also called an autotroph. A primary consumer will always receive its organic compounds by feeding off of autotrophs.

29. Global warming is threatening species such as the polar bear (*Ursus maritimus*). Which of the consequences below could be factors involved in decreasing populations of *Ursus maritimus*? [1]

I   Increased competition for resources as fewer seals are available

II Decrease in territory resulting in cross-breeding with brown bears (*Ursus arctos horribilis*)

III Increased contact with human villages

- ☐ A. I only
- ☐ B. I and II only
- ☐ C. I and III only
- ☐ D. I, II and III

> The lack of ice will cause a lack of food. This will affect survival rates because it causes polar bears to enter human towns, bringing them into conflict with humans.

> If their territory decreases, then polar bears may extend their habitat from sea ice to terrain. The species are similar enough to cross-breed and cause brown–polar hybrids.

30. The graphs below shows the mean monthly carbon dioxide measured at Mauna in Hawaii.

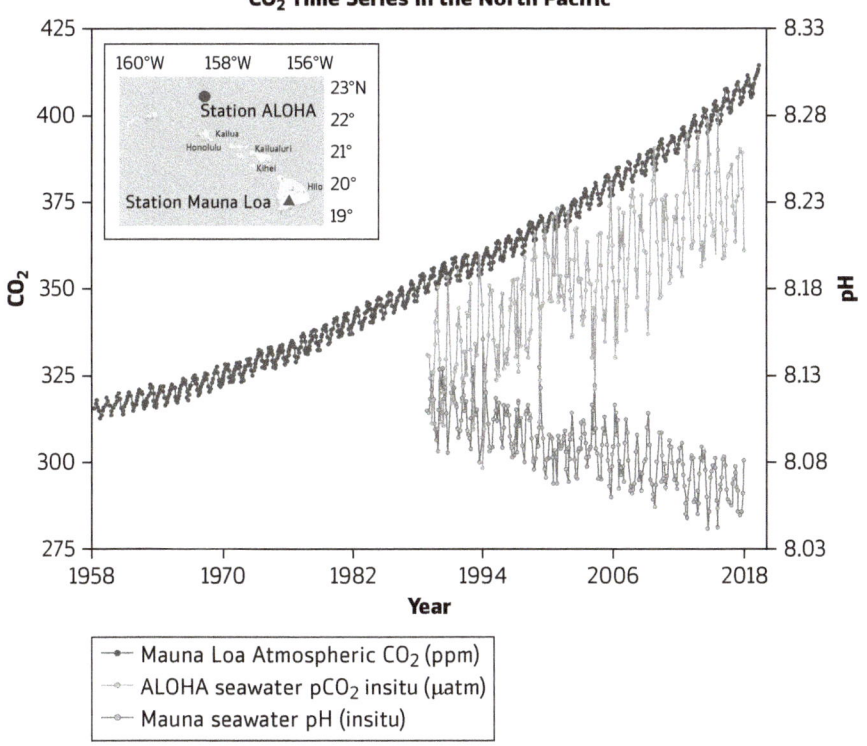

[© NOAA (Data: Mauna Loa (ftp://aftp.cmdl.noaa.gove/products/trends/co2/co2_mm_mlo.txt) ALOHA (http://soest.hawaii.edu))]

Which of the following conclusions can be made from the data in the graph?

I. The level of CO_2 is increasing between 1960 and 2020

II. There are seasonal variations in the data

III. Global warming causes CO_2 levels to change [1]

☐ A. I only

☐ B. II only

☐ C. I and II

☐ D. II and III

Set A

Paper 1B: Standard Level

- Answer all questions.
- Answers must be written on the answer lines provided. Continue on another piece of paper if you need to.
- A calculator is required for this paper.
- The maximum mark for paper 1B is **[25 marks]**

1. A study investigated the effect of pH (**A**) and temperature (**B**) on free lactase and on immobilized lactase encapsulated in a microsphere.

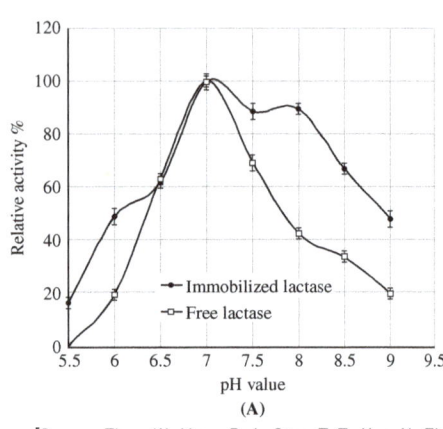
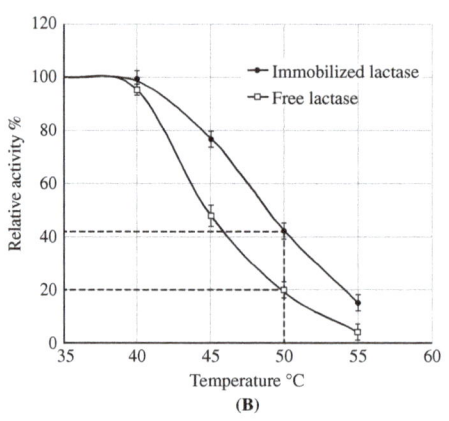

[Source: Zhao, W., Yang, R.-J., Qian, T.-T., Hua, X., Zhang, W.-B., Katiyo, W. 'Preparation of Novel Poly(hydroxyethyl methacrylate-co-glycidyl methacrylate)-Grafted Core-Shell Magnetic Chitosan Microspheres and Immobilization of Lactase.' Int. J. Mol. Sci. 2013, 14, 12073-12089.]

(a) Suggest **one** controlled variable for study **A**. [1]

(b) (i) Compare and contrast the effect of pH on immobilized lactase and free lactase. [2]

ANSWER ANALYSIS

State similarities and differences using comparatives, e.g. 'both', 'higher', 'lower', 'longer'. Make sure you are looking at the pH graph (**A**).

(ii) Suggest **one** advantage of immobilizing an enzyme such as lactase in industry. [1]

(c) The graph of the effect of pH on immobilized lactase activity does not allow for the determination of optimum pH. Using the information in graph (**A**), describe how the experiment could be extended to determine the optimum pH for immobilized lactase. [2]

> Here's an example of a knowledge question arising from the natural sciences area of knowledge as part of your TOK course.
>
> Perspectives: Does competition between scientists help or hinder the the production of knowledge?

(d) Suggest a possible research question for the data represented in graph (B). [2]

> Research questions should include the independent and dependent variables.

2. The trace below shows a student's breathing at rest and during light exercise.

[Spirometer trace: Volume of air in spirometer (dm³) vs Time (s), showing breathing at rest (0–55s) with region X indicated, and during exercise (55–100s) with region Y indicated.]

> This question is testing your understanding of AO1.

(a) State the independent variables. [1]

(b) Calculate the breathing rate per minute of the student at rest and during exercise. [1]

> **ANSWER ANALYSIS**
> Calculate the number of breaths in one minute.

(c) Calculate the mean tidal volume for the indicated breaths at rest (X) and during exercise (Y). [2]

> **ANSWER ANALYSIS**
> You can just measure the distance between the middle of the parallel lines, or you can add each one up at a time. Either way you need to check the scale on the Y-axis.

(d) Suggest a reason why the trace slopes downwards more steeply during exercise than at rest. [1]

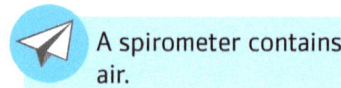
A spirometer contains air.

(e) Suggest the effect of exercise on the expiratory reserve volume. [1]

3. Coral calcification is the rate at which corals can build their calcium carbonate skeletons. Human activities are increasing atmospheric CO_2 levels which are causing increased partial pressure of CO_2 in oceans. As a result, reef-building corals could become unable to undergo calcification.

A study used mesocosms to investigate the effect of increasing the partial pressure of CO_2 levels in oceans from 460 μatmr to 789 μatmr on the common calcifying coral reef organisms.

Calcification of coral in mesocosm

[Bar chart: y-axis "Rate of calcification of coral (mmol $CaCO_3$ m^{-2} h^{-1})" from 0 to 20; x-axis "Partial pressure of CO_2 in seawater (μatmr)"; bar at 460 (+/−16) ≈ 16; bar at 789 (+/−9) ≈ 9]

[Source: Data Copyright 2005 by the American Geophysical Union.]

(a) State the dependent variable. [1]

(b) Suggest a controlled variable in the experiment. [1]

(c) Determine the effect of increasing the partial pressure of CO_2 in seawater on the rate of calcification of coral. [1]

(d) Other than controlling variables, outline an advantage of using a mesocosm rather than monitoring coral in the ocean. [1]

Remember, the dependent variable is always on the y-axis. Remember to include units.

What should be kept the same in the two mesocosms to ensure results are valid?

ANSWER ANALYSIS

Use the graph and look at the two partial pressures and their corresponding rate of calcification.

Why is the model of an environment used?

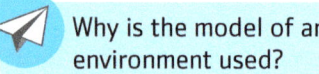
What limitations does the model environment have?

(e) State a disadvantage of the mesocosm. **[1]**

(f) Suggest an effect of calcification of coral on marine ecosystems. **[1]**

4. The image shows a section of a tobacco leaf chloroplast.

   > Measure the scale bar with a ruler in mm. Multiply by 1000 to convert to micrometers.

   (a) Calculate the magnification of the chloroplast. **[1]**

   > Magnification of an image is equal to the size of the image / actual size. Make sure the same units are used when dividing!

   (b) State with a reason the type of microscope used to take this image. **[1]**

   It is estimated that chloroplasts contain 2,000 to 5,000 proteins.

   (c) Suggest the function of the ribosomes found in chloroplasts. **[1]**

   > What is the function of free-floating ribosomes in eukaryotic cells?

   (d) Suggest a technique used to produce 3 dimensional images of protein structures. **[1]**

   (e) State one advantage for compartmentalizing the cytoplasm into organelles. **[1]**

Set A

Paper 2: Standard Level

Set your timer for **1 hour and 30 minutes**

- The maximum mark for this examination paper is **[50 marks]**
- **Section A** - answer ALL the questions
- **Section B** - answer **one** question
- A calculator is needed for this paper

Section A

1. Bovine tuberculosis (TB) is a disease that can be transferred from wildlife hosts to other mammalian species. The infection of livestock (such as cows – *Bos taurus*) results in severe economic losses from death and disease.

   TB is caused by the bacteria *Mycobacterium bovis* and is spread from wild animals such as the Australian brushtail possum (*Trichosurus vulpecula*). TB can be transmitted to humans as well as to other animals.

   (a) State the domain the infected cows belong to. **[1]**

   ....

   > The paragraph at the top of Q1 tells you some basic information about the topic. Annotate in the margin the area of the syllabus that the paragraph loosely relates to. This will help you later. It may link more than one area – for example, human biology, diabetes and stem cells. This will focus your mind for the later parts of Q1.

    ANSWER ANALYSIS

   The first question is a straightforward question such as reading off a graph or a **state** question in which you need to recall/read off the one correct answer. The domain it belongs to is Eukaryota. You don't need to justify your answer at all. Just a one-word answer will get you the mark here. If it is a read off the graph question then check you are reading off the correct line/bar/scale.

   ⓘ Don't get confused with the genus. The genus the cows belong to is *Bos*.

    ANSWER ANALYSIS

   The phrase 'transmitted to humans' links with defence against disease. The key words of 'disease' and 'bacteria' also do this.

   (b) Use information from the text above to identify the treatment for humans who have contracted bovine tuberculosis. **[1]**

   ....

   ....

    ANSWER ANALYSIS

   You might consider vaccinations; however, vaccination would not be appropriate as the person has already contracted bovine TB. As bovine TB is caused by bacteria, think about the treatments for bacterial diseases.

   A study in New Zealand investigated if the human BCG vaccination was effective in preventing TB in wild possums. An oral vaccine in food was delivered to one group of wild possums. A second control group did not receive the vaccine. Initial vaccinations were applied in November–December 2004 and the animals were tagged and released back into the wild. Every two months for two years the scientists recaptured the animals and tested them for the presence of TB. The vaccine was reapplied to recaptured possums at six-month intervals.

The graph below shows trapped possums with TB (black) and without TB (grey). Graph (*a*) shows the control group and Graph (*b*) shows the vaccinated group.

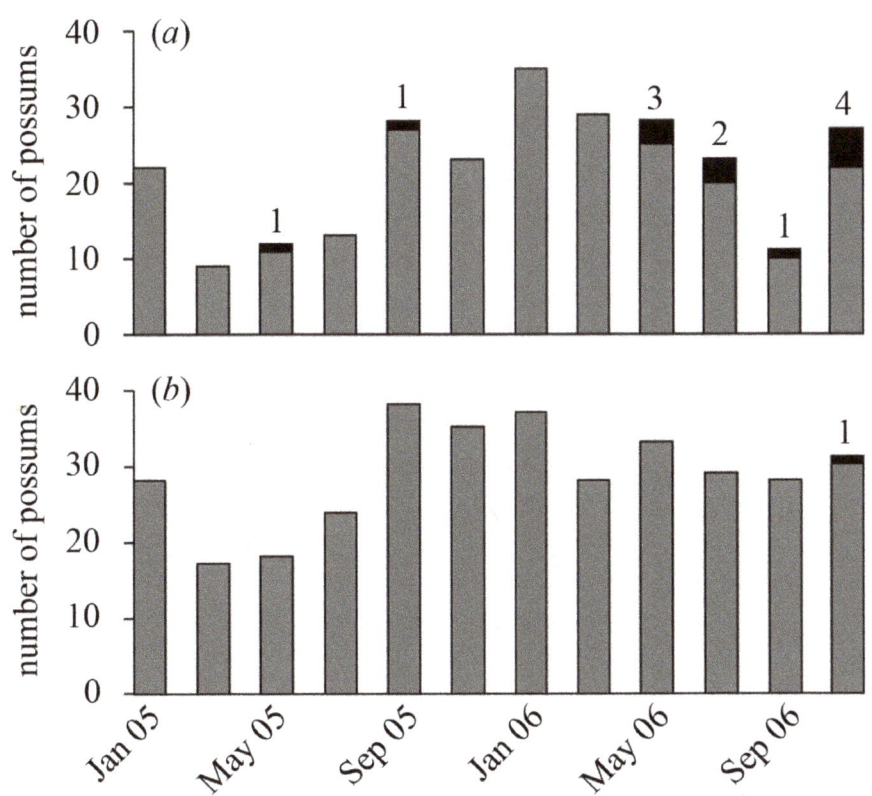

[Source: Tompkins D. M., Ramsey D. S. L., Cross M. L., Aldwell F. E., de Lisle G. W. and Buddle B. M. 2009. 'Oral vaccination reduces the incidence of tuberculosis in free-living brushtail possums.' Proc. R. Soc. B.2762987–2995 http://doi.org/10.1098/rspb.2009.0414.]

(c) Identify the month and year when the first case of TB was identified in the trial. [1]

(d) Calculate the percentage of possums with TB in November 2006 in the:
   (i) control group [1]

   (ii) vaccinated group. [1]

ANSWER ANALYSIS

The text tells you that the black boxes are TB. Read down to see the month and year. Don't forget to put both the month **and** the year.

IDENTIFY

Here, identify means that you need to give the correct answer from a range of possible answers (i.e. from Jan 05 to Sept 06).

Use a ruler to draw a horizontal line across from the bar to the axis and ensure you accurately read off the scale (to nearest mm). Then work out what the mm equates to on the scale. In this example 10 possums = 10 mm so each mm = 1 possum.

ANSWER ANALYSIS

This question requires you to look at the correct graph. The information above the graph states that the top graph is the control group. You then need to work out the last column on the right is November 2006 as the months are only labelled Jan, May, Sep, but the bars are Jan, Mar, May, July, Sep, Nov. Percentage with TB in the control group in November is 4 out of 27. The percentage = 4/27 × 100%.

ANSWER ANALYSIS

This involves looking at the bottom graph. For (ii) vaccinated group 1/31 × 100%.

(e) Based on the graph, compare and contrast the infection rates with TB in the control and vaccinated groups. **[2]**

COMPARE AND CONTRAST

In a compare and contrast question, you need to give similarities and differences. Ensure you use the words 'both' and some comparatives such as 'higher' or 'more'.

ANSWER ANALYSIS

Look at the graphs for similarities and differences. You also need to be clear which group you are referring to when looking at differences. It helps to put the data from the graph axes in to help you with the answer, but you should not just state the data; rather you need to compare it, for example - higher/lower/earlier/later/more/less/twice/half, etc. You need to make two points for a 2-mark compare and contrast question. If looking for similarities and there are error bars that significantly overlap, there is no signicant difference between the data. It helps to bullet point your answers. There is more than one possible correct answer for each mark.

A second long-term study investigated whether BCG-vaccinated calves would still be protected against *Mycobacterium bovis* two-and-a-half years after vaccination. The IFN-γ TB test responses measure the amount of interferon gamma antibody in response to the TB antigens.

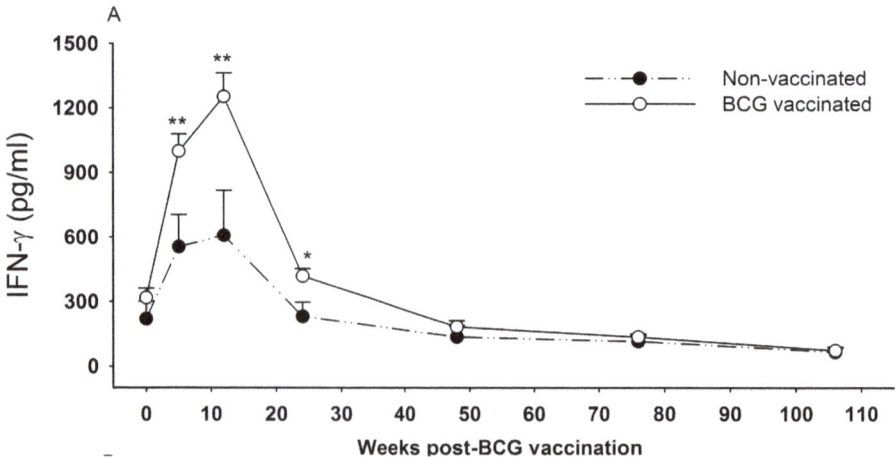

[Source: Parlane, N.A, Shu, D., Subharat, S., Wedlock, D.N., Rehm, B.H.A., (2014) 'Revaccination of Cattle with Bacille Calmette-Guérin Two Years after First Vaccination when Immunity Has Waned, Boosted Protection against Challenge with Mycobacterium bovis'. PLoS ONE 9(9): e106519. doi:10.1371/journal.pone.0106519.]

The words 'interferon gamma antibody' show the question is linked to the original defence against disease question, looking at long-term immunity from vaccination. It is linked to the second study as it is still about TB but is now testing the livestock the possums transmit the TB to. It is measuring the antibody level IFN (this is given in the text).

(f) State the highest amount of IFN-γ in non-vaccinated calves. **[1]**

ANSWER ANALYSIS

A second graph is often given in Q1 which is a different type of graph from the first. It could also be a table or chart. In this case it's a line graph. The **state** question simply wants you to read off the answer from the correct line by using the key.

(g) Use the graph to outline the evidence that vaccination has the potential to prevent TB in cattle. **[2]**

(h) Using **all** the data, evaluate the use of vaccination to prevent the spread of TB to domestic livestock. **[3]**

2. The bluebell *Hyacinthoides non-scripta* is a woodland plant found in woodland in the United Kingdom. The diagram shows a flower from a hybrid bluebell produced from *Hyacinthoides non-scripta* and the Spanish bluebell, *Hyacinthoides hispanica*.

(a) Label structures I, II and III. **[2]**

(b) Suggest, with a reason, how the plant is pollinated. **[2]**

ANSWER ANALYSIS

When evaluating data, you should look at the sample sizes and error bars. If the sample size is small or the study is over a short time, there may not be enough data for valid statistical analysis. If error bars are large there is a lot of variation in the data. Use knowledge or data or make a deduction from the data.

The vaccinated line graph needs to be compared to the non-vaccinated line graph.

ANSWER ANALYSIS

Here you need to look back at the topic in the introduction to the question for clues as well as using all the data in the different parts of the question. You will also need to use your knowledge about the topics covered such as vaccines and immunity to develop a conclusion. Be clear which graph or study the data has come from. Remember it links back to the text information at the start of the question and the syllabus link that you made.

This questions tests your understanding of AO1. Make sure you can label the male (anther and filament) and female (stigma, style, ovary) parts of a flower.

Brightly coloured flowers attract insects. How could an insect increase pollination between flowers?

(c) Outline the use of the binomial system of nomenclature in categorizing *Hyacinthoides non-scripta* and *Hyacinthoides hispanica*. **[2]**

> It is a system of classification introduced by Carl Linnaeus. What do the two (bi) name (nom) words represent?

3. (a) Amylopectin and cellulose are both carbohydrates found in plants. State what type of carbohydrate amylose and cellulose are. **[1]**

> Carbohydrates could be monosaccharides, disaccharides or polysaccharides.

(b) Identify the bond formed when glucose monomers join. **[1]**

> Although it is a covalent bond, this question specifically refers to joining of glucose monomers, so you need to be more specific than 'covalent'.

(c) Distinguish between the structure of a cellulose and an amylopectin molecule. **[3]**

> For 3(c), you can use a table or use comparatives. Look for at least **three** differences. Think about the monomers they are constructed from, the orientation of the molecules, the shape and the type of bonding.

ANSWER ANALYSIS

For 3(d), you need to make at least two points, one for starch and one for cellulose.

(d) Outline one way in which the amylopectin and the cellulose molecule are each adapted for their function. **[2]**

4. The table shows the approximate percentages of each base in the genetic material of different species.

Organism	Percentage of each base			
	%A	%G	%C	%T
Octopus	32	18	18	32
Human	30	20	20	30
Grasshopper	29			
Yeast	31	19	19	31
Bacteriophage φX174	24	23	22	31

[Source: Data from Erwin Chargaff's 1952 data, Elson D, Chargaff E (1952). "On the deoxyribonucleic acid content of sea urchin gametes". *Experientia*. 8 (4): 143–145.]

(a) State the percentage of G, C and T in the grasshopper's genetic material. **[1]**

G .... C .... T ....

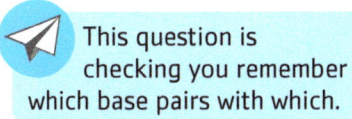
This question is checking you remember which base pairs with which.

(b) Suggest why humans and yeast are so different despite having similar percentages of bases in their DNA. **[2]**

....

....

....

....

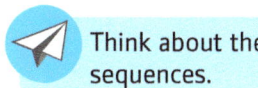
Think about the sequences.

(c) Use the table to explain the type of genetic material the bacteriophage virus has. **[2]**

....

....

....

....

Single-stranded DNA contains all four bases joined without complementary base pairing. RNA does not contain thymine but contains uracil.

5. The image shows a karyogram from a person with Edwards' syndrome.

(a) Identify, with a reason, the sex of the person in the karyogram. [1]

> The sex chromosomes are shown at the bottom right of the karyogram.

(b) State the stage and type of cell division used to make this karyogram. [1]

(c) State the name of the condition resulting in the development of Edwards' Syndrome. [1]

> There should only be two homologous copies of each chromosome.

Section B

Answer **one** question from a choice of two.

One additional mark is available for the construction of your answer.

6. Developments in the understanding of DNA have revolutionized medicine in the 21st century.

    (a) Draw a labelled diagram of a DNA nucleotide. [3]

    > Here's an example of a knowledge question arising from the natural sciences area of knowledge as part of your TOK course.
    >
    > Perspectives: How can it be that scientific knowledge changes over time?

    > Clearly draw a pentose sugar with a phosphate and base. Label with phosphate, deoxyribose sugar and nitrogenous base.

     This question tests your understanding of AO1. You need to demonstrate knowledge and comprehension of specified content.

    (b) Outline the stages involved in synthesis of mRNA from DNA. [4]

    > **OUTLINE**
    >
    > Give a brief account or summary.

(c) Explain the inheritance of sickle cell disease and the benefits of genetic screening of embryos in parents who are heterozygous for the trait. **[8]**

> Consider how a mutation in the haemoglobin gene affects red blood cells.

> What is the chance that two heterozygous individuals have an offspring with sickle cell disease?

7. The composition and processes of blood play crucial roles in health and disease.

   (a) State three substances transported in blood plasma. **[3]**

(b) Outline the coagulation cascade that occurs in blood and its significance in blood clotting. [5]

> The cascade is a metabolic pathway starting with clotting factors and ending with fibrin. You may find drawing a flow diagram useful in your answer.

(c) Explain the inheritance of haemophilia. [7]

> **EXPLAIN**
> Give a detailed account including the reasons or causes.

> State the type of inheritance. Identify the alleles involved. It is useful to draw a genetic cross between a carrier female and normal male, then identify the genotypes and phenotypes of the offspring.

Set B

Are you ready to tackle Set B? There are fewer helpful tips and suggestions for this set so make sure you have done some revision before you try out these two papers.

Paper 1A: Standard Level

Set your timer for 1 hour 30 minutes **[Paper 1A and Paper 1B]**.

- Each question is worth **[1]** mark.
- For each question, choose the answer you consider to be the best and put a tick next to it in the book.
- A calculator is required for this paper.
- The maximum mark for paper 1A is **[30 marks]**.

> In the real exam, you will be writing your answers on a separate answer sheet provided.

1. Which property of water explains its use as a coolant? [1]

    ☐ A. Adhesion

    ☐ B. High specific heat capacity

    ☐ C. High latent heat of vaporization

    ☐ D. Cohesion

> **High latent heat of vaporization** refers to the energy required to evaporate liquid. **High specific heat capacity** refers to the energy needed to raise the temperature of water.

Water is polar. **Adhesion** is water attracted to other polar molecules. **Cohesion** is water attracted to other water molecules.

> The question requires DNA to be compared with RNA.
> DNA is arranged into a double helix and is made up of deoxyribonucleotides. It has the bases ATGC.

2. Which row is the correct comparison between eukaryotic DNA and RNA? [1]

		DNA	RNA
☐	A.	Pentose sugars have a hydroxyl (OH) group on carbon 2	Pentose sugars have no hydroxyl (OH) group on carbon 2
☐	B.	Genetic material contains bases A U C G	Genetic material contains bases A T C U
☐	C.	Single-stranded	Double-stranded
☐	D.	Double-stranded	Single-stranded

3. Which molecule could be hydrolysed into glucose? [1]

☐ A.

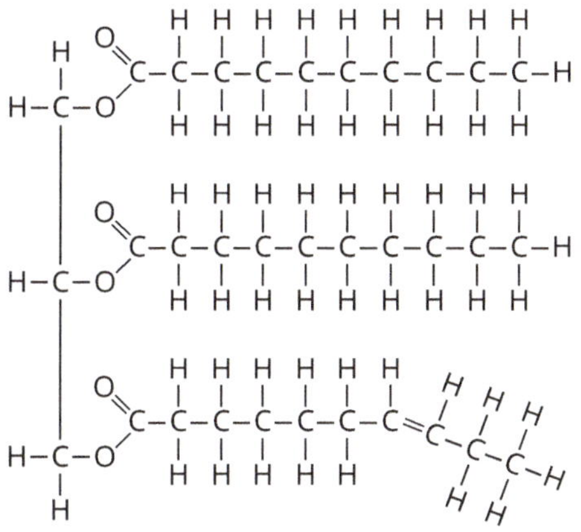

☐ B.

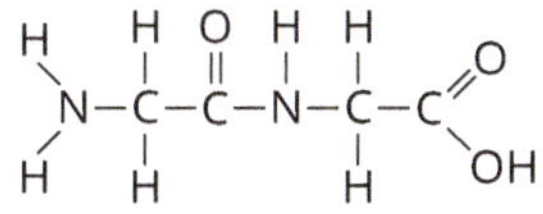

☐ C.

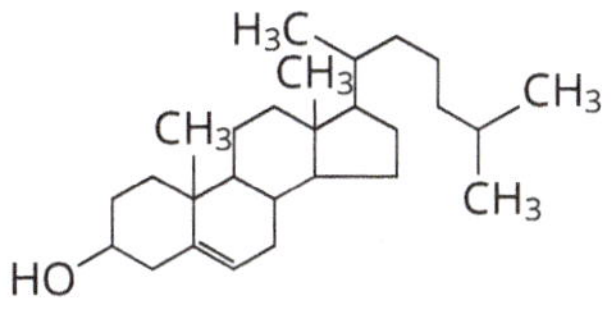

☐ D.

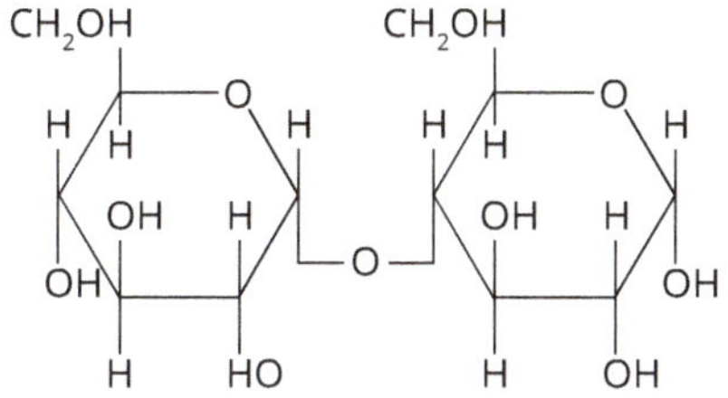

A. Is a triglyceride – three fatty acid chains and one glycerol joined by an ester bond.

B. Is a dipeptide – two amino acids joined by a peptide bond.

C. Is a steroid – it contains covalently bonded carbon rings.

D. Is maltose – made up of two glucose monomers joined by a glycosidic bond.

A condensation reaction removes water to join monomers.

A hydrolysis reaction requires water to split a molecule into its monomers.

4. The diagram below shows the structure of oleic acid.

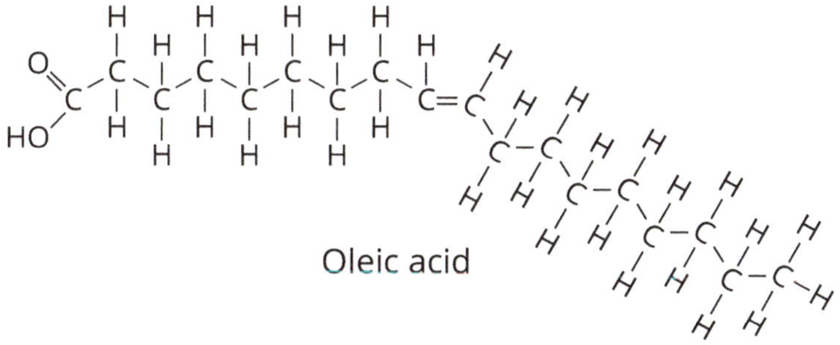

Oleic acid

What type of fatty acid is oleic acid? [1]

☐ A. It is a trans-fatty acid

☐ B. It is monounsaturated

☐ C. It is saturated

☐ D. It is polyunsaturated

The hydrocarbon chain contains a carbon to carbon double bond (C=C). Both hydrogen atoms are on the same side of the C=C.

5. A section of a molecule is shown below. Identify the molecule. [1]

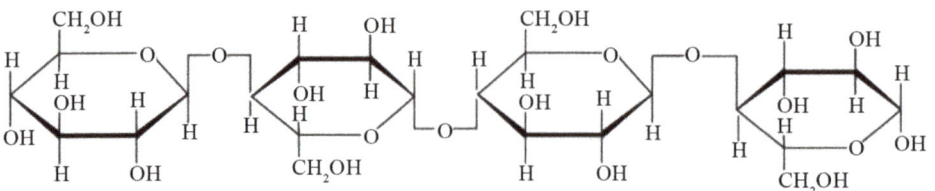

- ☐ A. Glycogen
- ☐ B. Amylopectin
- ☐ C. Amylose
- ☐ D. Cellulose

> Cellulose is a polysaccharide made up of alternatively oriented beta glucose. It is unbranched.

> Amylose and amylopectin are both forms of starch. They are made up of alpha glucose. Amylose is unbranched and only contains 1–4 glycosidic bonds whereas amylopectin is branched and contains 1–4 and 1–6 glycosidic bonds

> Glycogen is how glucose is stored in muscles and the liver. It is similar in structure to amylose but has more branches. It contains 1–4 glycosidic bonds only.

6. The gene for the alpha chain of haemoglobin codes for 141 amino acids. How many peptide bonds does it contain? [1]

- ☐ A. 423
- ☐ B. 47
- ☐ C. 140
- ☐ D. 282

> There is always one fewer peptide bond than amino acids.

7. The graph below shows the effect of substrate concentration on the rate of reaction of an enzyme. What has happened at X? [1]

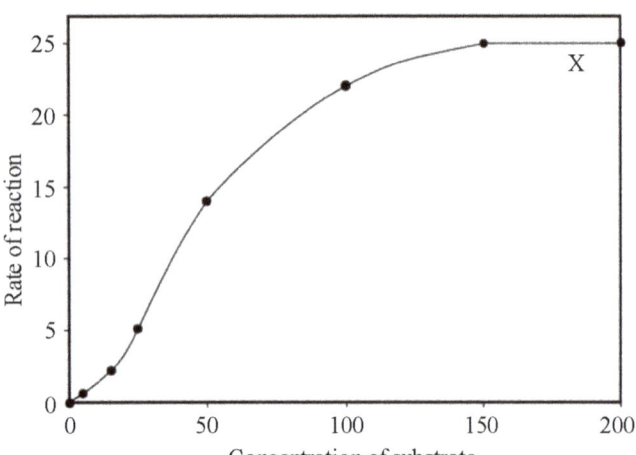

- ☐ A. The enzyme is saturated with the substrate, so the enzyme is working at its maximum rate
- ☐ B. The reaction has finished
- ☐ C. Some enzymes have been denatured so the reaction has slowed down
- ☐ D. The enzyme has reached its optimum pH

> Read the X-axis label. Has the reaction finished or is it going at its fastest?

8. The graph below shows how temperature affected the rate of photosynthesis in three experiments. What conclusion can be drawn from the graph? [1]

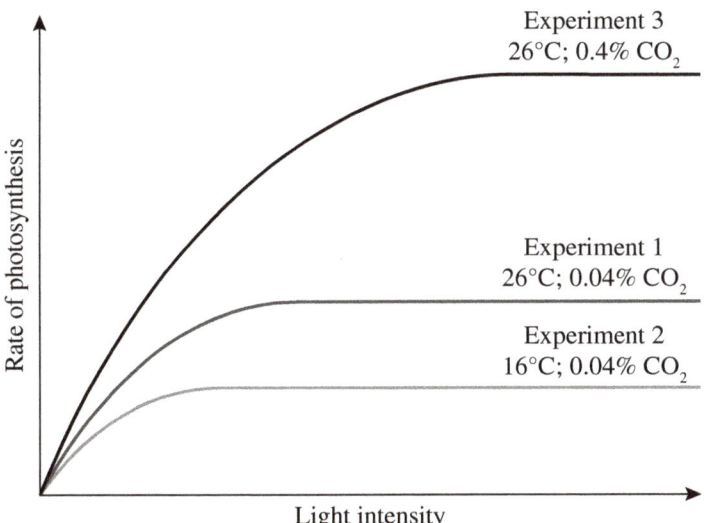

- ☐ A. At high light intensities light is the limiting factor
- ☐ B. In Experiment 1 at high light intensities the limiting factor is temperature
- ☐ C. In Experiment 1 at high light intensities the limiting factor is carbon dioxide
- ☐ D. Temperature is not a limiting factor in Experiment 2

> A limiting factor can be identified if an increase in it causes an increase in photosynthesis. At low light intensities light is a limiting factor. If the light increases then so does the rate of photosynthesis.

ANSWER ANALYSIS

Compare Experiments 1 and 2: there is one variable that has increased. What does this tell you about the limiting factor in Experiment 1? Now compare Experiments 2 and 3.

> Why would comparing Experiments 1 and 3 not help to identify limiting factors?

9. What is the correct definition for translation and where does it occur? Choose the correct row. [1]

	Location	Definition
☐ A.	Nucleus	DNA is used as a template to make mRNA
☐ B.	Nucleus	mRNA is used as a template to make proteins
☐ C.	Cytoplasm	DNA is used as a template to make mRNA
☐ D.	Cytoplasm	mRNA is used as a template to make proteins

> **Transcription** is the copying of the DNA code into mRNA.

> **Translation** is the decoding of mRNA into a sequence of amino acids.

10. Below is a section of DNA in the beta globin gene Hb^A that has mutated to form a different allele Hb^S.

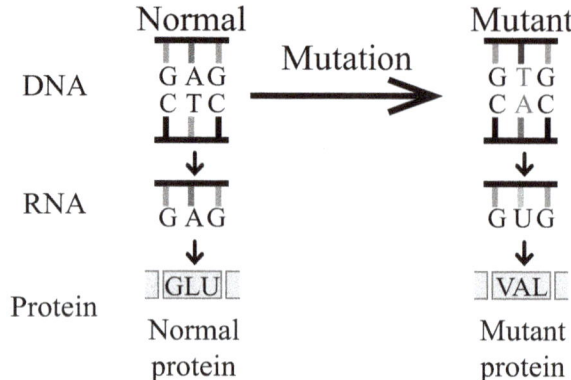

Which statement is the correct explanation and consequence of the mutation GAG → GTG? [1]

☐ A. Non-disjunction of chromosome 21 in meiosis causing Down syndrome

☐ B. Base substitution of A to T resulting in amino acid valine causing sickle cell disease

☐ C. Base substitution of T to A resulting in amino acid glutamic acid causing sickle cell disease

☐ D. Non-disjunction of chromosome 18 in meiosis causing Down syndrome

> Haemoglobin is found in red blood cells and transports oxygen. It is a conjugated protein consisting of four polypeptides (two alpha globin and two beta globin), each attached to iron haem prosthetic groups.

> A base substitution mutation (A to T) on the 6th codon of the sense strand for beta globin results in the normal codon GAG being replaced with GTG. The mutated codon is transcribed to produce a GUG sequence in the mRNA, rather than the normal GAG sequence. During translation, the normal GAG anticodon codes for the polar glutamic acid, whereas GUG codes for the less polar valine. As a result, the beta haemoglobin becomes sickle shaped in low oxygen concentrations, resulting in sickle cell disease, chronic fatigue and severe pain.

> The two alleles are co-dominant: Hb^A is the normal allele and Hb^S is the sickle cell allele. If a person has sickle cell disease, they have the genotype Hb^SHb^S. If they are a carrier of sickle cell disease, they have the genotype Hb^AHb^S and have resistance to malaria. Hb^AHb^A is the normal phenotype.

11. The gene that codes for a polypeptide includes the following base sequence:

GACCTCATTGGA

What is the base sequence of the mRNA molecule coded from **this** template? [1]

☐ A. GACCTCATTGGA

☐ B. GACCUCAUUGGA

☐ C. CTGGAGTAACCT

☐ D. CUGGAGUAACCU

> If this sequence is copied by complementary base pairing (T–A, A–U, G–C, C–G) the mRNA will contain uracil instead of thymine.

12. This image shows a giant algae *Acetabularia mediterranea*.

Why is it an exception to cell theory? [1]

☐ A. It does not come from pre-existing cells

☐ B. It only has one nucleus

☐ C. It is made up of 1 cell 100 mm in size

☐ D. It has hyphae

13. Which of the following is an example of osmosis? [1]

☐ A. Loss of water from the stomata of leaves

☐ B. Movement of water into a cell from a hypertonic solution

☐ C. Evaporation of sweat from the surface of skin

☐ D. Loss of water from a cell in a hypertonic solution

> In this question you need to know the three principles of cell theory:
> - All organisms are made of cells
> - Cells are the smallest **unit** of life
> - Cells come from pre-existing cells.

> Which way will water move between a cell and hypertonic solution?

> Remember, osmosis is the movement of water from a dilute (hypotonic) solution to a concentrated (hypertonic) solution **across a partially permeable membrane**.

14. This table shows the concentration of sodium and potassium ions in red blood cells and plasma. Which type of transport explains these concentrations? [1]

Concentration of ions (mM dm^{-3})		
Ions	Inside red blood cells	Inside plasma
Potassium	100	4
Sodium	10	150
Chloride	50	100

[Source: Adapted from Figure 1 in Ron Milo & Rob Phillips, 'Cell Biology by the Numbers', (*Garland Science*, 2015), p. 130]

☐ A. Potassium moves into the red blood cells by diffusion

☐ B. Potassium moves into the red blood cells by active transport

☐ C. Sodium moves out of the red blood cells by diffusion

☐ D. Chloride moves into the red blood cells by active transport

Diffusion is the movement of particles from a high to low concentration.

Active transport is the movement of particles from a low to high concentration, requiring energy.

15. The image shows the number of chromosomes in a karyotype of a mouse cell following mitosis. What is the number of chromosomes in a gamete? [1]

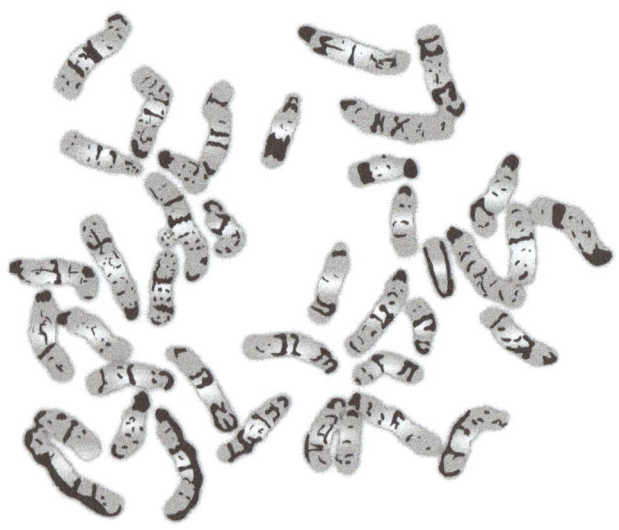

☐ A. 20

☐ B. 40

☐ C. 10

☐ D. 15

The diploid number is shown in the karyotype. A gamete or sex cell has the haploid number.

16. The four micrographs show different phases of meiosis. What is the correct order? [1]

1   2   3   4

- ☐ A. 3,1,4,2
- ☐ B. 1,3,4,2
- ☐ C. 3,1,2,4
- ☐ D. 1,3,2,4

17. Which of the four bears are the most closely related? [1]

I — *Ursus maritimus*
III — *Ursus arctos*
II — *Ailuropoda melanoleuca*
IV — *Phascolarctos cinereus*

- ☐ A. I and II
- ☐ B. II and IV
- ☐ C. I and III
- ☐ D. III and IV

18. Which factor reduces the rate of transpiration? [1]

- ☐ A. High temperature
- ☐ B. High humidity
- ☐ C. High wind
- ☐ D. High light level

> ❗ The hierarchy of taxa: Domain, Kingdom, Phylum, Class, Order, Family, Genus, Species.

> 🛈 Species of a similar type are grouped into the same genus.

> 🛈 The binomial name gives the genus and species name.

> 🛈 Transpiration increases if the water vapour diffuses more quickly from the leaf. A high temperature increases the kinetic energy of the water vapour molecules so diffusion will be faster. Wind will reduce the water molecules on the outside of the leaf so the concentration gradient between the inside and outside will be steeper and diffusion faster. A high light level will mean stomata are open so transpiration increases. High humidity will increase the water vapour outside the stomata, which will make the concentration gradient shallower so diffusion will be slower.

19. Which is the correct statement for gas exchange in the lungs? [1]

☐ A. Oxygen diffuses into the capillaries and carbon dioxide diffuses into the alveoli

☐ B. Oxygen diffuses into the alveoli and carbon dioxide diffuses into the capillaries

☐ C. Oxygen and carbon dioxide move against their concentration gradient by active transport

☐ D. Oxygen and carbon dioxide move down their concentration gradient by osmosis

> Diffusion is the movement of particles from a high to low concentration.

20. Which row contains the correct statements about arteries, veins and capillaries? [1]

	Artery	Capillary	Vein
☐ A.	Thick muscular wall with elastic fibres and muscle	Wall one cell thick	Valves present
☐ B.	Always oxygenated	Gas exchange occurs here	Always deoxygenated
☐ C.	Valves present	Always oxygenated	Thick muscular wall with elastic fibres and muscle
☐ D.	Always deoxygenated	Valves present	Wall one cell thick

> **!** Ve**in**s go **in**to the heart. **A**rteries go **a**way from the heart.

> Valves are present in veins to stop the slow-moving low-pressure blood from flowing backwards.

> Capillary walls are one cell thick to allow a short diffusion distance for fast diffusion.

> Arteries are usually oxygenated but there are exceptions. For example, the pulmonary artery carries deoxygenated blood from the heart to the lungs and the umbilical artery carries deoxygenated blood from the fetus through the umbilical cord.

21. Which statement is true about the antibiotic streptomycin? [1]

☐ A. It can be used to treat the influenza virus

☐ B. It damages eukaryotic cells without damaging the host cells

☐ C. It will not work on viruses because viruses do not have their own metabolism

☐ D. It kills all types of bacteria

> Antibiotics work by attacking part of bacterial cells that are not present in eukaryotic cells, such as the peptidoglycan cell wall. This means they kill the prokaryotes without harming the eukaryotes.

> Viruses do not have their own metabolism so they invade hosts cells. As a result, viruses can't be destroyed without damaging the host cell. This means antibiotics will not work on viruses.

22. Which hormones in the menstrual cycle are part of a negative feedback mechanism? [1]

☐ A. LH stimulates progesterone
☐ B. Oestrogen inhibits FSH
☐ C. LH inhibits progesterone
☐ D. Oestrogen stimulates LH

23. A woman who has two alleles for haemophilia has a child with a man who does not have the alleles for haemophilia. What is the probability that their child will have haemophilia? [1]

☐ A. 0% for a girl and 50% for a boy
☐ B. 75% haemophilia and 25% no haemophilia
☐ C. 50% no haemophilia and 50% haemophilia
☐ D. 0% for a girl and 100% for a boy

> Haemophilia is a sex-linked recessive disorder.
> X^h = hemophiliac allele, X^H = normal allele, Y = male chromosome
> Phenotypes affected female × normal male
> Genotypes X^hX^h X^HY
> Draw a Punnett grid and then look at the sex of the children and whether or not they will have hemophilia.

24. Use the following pedigree chart to deduce the form of inheritance. [1]

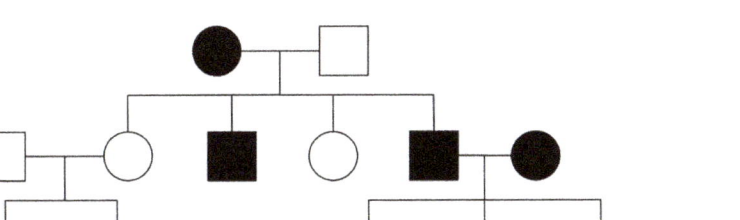

☐ A. Autosomal dominant
☐ B. Co-dominant
☐ C. Sex-linked dominant
☐ D. Sex-linked recessive

> An **autosomal trait** will have a similar number of affected males (squares) and females (circles).
> A **sex-linked (X-linked) trait** has significantly more male descendants affected than females.
> A **dominant trait** must have an affected parent in every generation whereas a recessive trait can have unaffected parents having an affected child.

25. What is the name for the combination of alleles in an individual organism? [1]

☐ A. Genome
☐ B. Karyogram
☐ C. Gene
☐ D. Genotype

> **Gene**: an inherited length of DNA that influences a characteristic. Genes have a specific location on a chromosome called a locus. Different forms of a gene are called alleles.
> **Genome**: all the genetic information of an organism.
> **Karyotype**: the number and type of chromosomes in an individual. A **karyogram** is an image of these chromosomes arranged into homologous pairs from largest to smallest with the sex chromosomes last.
> **Genotype**: the particular combination of alleles for a particular gene.

26. Which of the following is **not** evidence for evolution? [1]

    ☐ A. Selective breeding of domesticated animals

    ☐ B. Homologous structures

    ☐ C. Industrial melanism

    ☐ D. The inheritance of acquired characteristics.

27. A transect was set up to investigate how the population of a species changed in a woodland. What type of statistical test should be used to find out if the distance into the woodland affects bluebell distribution? [1]

   ☐ A. Chi-squared

   ☐ B. T-Test

   ☐ C. Correlation coefficient

   ☐ D. Standard deviation

> **Selective breeding** or artificial selection occurs when humans have bred animals or plants with desirable traits together. The selection of traits has led to extreme differences in phenotypes such as the huge variety in dog breeds and the large differences between dog breeds and their wild ancestor the wolf.

> - A **chi-squared** test is used to determine if counted observed values match expected predicted values.
> - A **t-test** compares the means of two populations to determine if there is a significant difference between them.
> - **Correlation** such as Spearman rank or Pearson look for a relationship between two variables.
> - **Standard deviation** looks at the variation of the data around the mean. 95% of data lies within one standard deviation of the mean. A small standard deviation suggests the data shows little variation.

28. The diagram shows an Antarctic food web. Krill are a keystone species. Global rises in temperature have reduced the amount of sea ice, which young krill shelter and feed under.

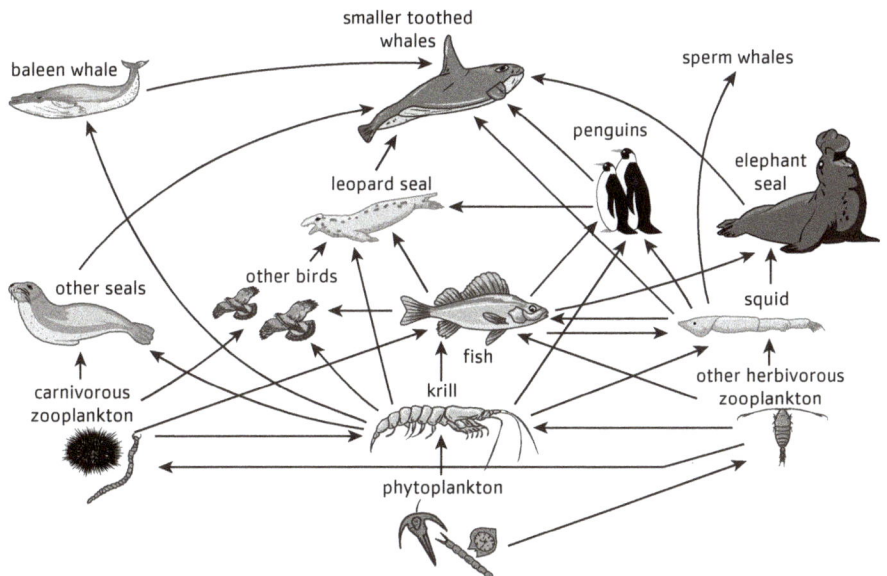

Which of the following statements is the most likely result of the diminishing sea ice? [1]

- ☐ A. Baleen whale decrease
- ☐ B. Phytoplankton decrease
- ☐ C. Herbivorous zooplankton decrease
- ☐ D. Krill numbers increase

29. Which statement is **not** true about food chains? [1]

- ☐ A. Energy enters as light and is lost as heat from respiration
- ☐ B. Approximately 10% of the energy is transferred between trophic levels
- ☐ C. Energy is transferred from one trophic level to the next by feeding
- ☐ D. Energy is recycled but matter flows through the ecosystem

30. The Venus flytrap *Dionaea muscipula* is a photosynthetic plant that lives on nutrient-depleted soil. It obtains its energy from sunlight but gets its minerals from insects it traps. What is its mode of nutrition? [1]

- ☐ A. Autotroph only
- ☐ B. Autotroph and heterotroph
- ☐ C. Heterotroph only
- ☐ D. Parasite and heterotroph

> An autotroph or producer makes organic food from inorganic substances, usually by photosynthesis.

> A primary consumer obtains its energy by feeding on autotrophs.

> A top carnivore is at the top of the food chain.

> Not all energy is transferred to the next trophic level. Think about where energy goes besides growth.

> Remember, a **heterotroph** obtains its organic matter from other organisms whereas **autotrophs** synthesize their own organic matter from inorganic molecules. Heterotrophs include **consumers, detritivores** and **saprotrophs**.

Set B

Paper 1B: Standard Level

- Answer all the questions.
- Answers must be written on the answer lines provided. Continue on another piece of paper if you need to.
- A calculator is required for this paper.
- The maximum mark for paper 1B is **[25 marks]**.

1. A student investigated osmosis in 9 potato (*Solanum tuberosum*) cubes and 9 sweet potato (*Ipomoea batatas*) cubes in different concentrations of salt solution. They measured 1 gram of sweet potato and potato. The student then placed them into test tubes containing 20 cm^3 of various concentrations of salt solutions (NaCl). After 1 hour the final mass was recorded by removing the potato/sweet potato and putting it on the scales. The percentage change in mass was plotted against the concentration of salt solution for both potato and sweet potato.

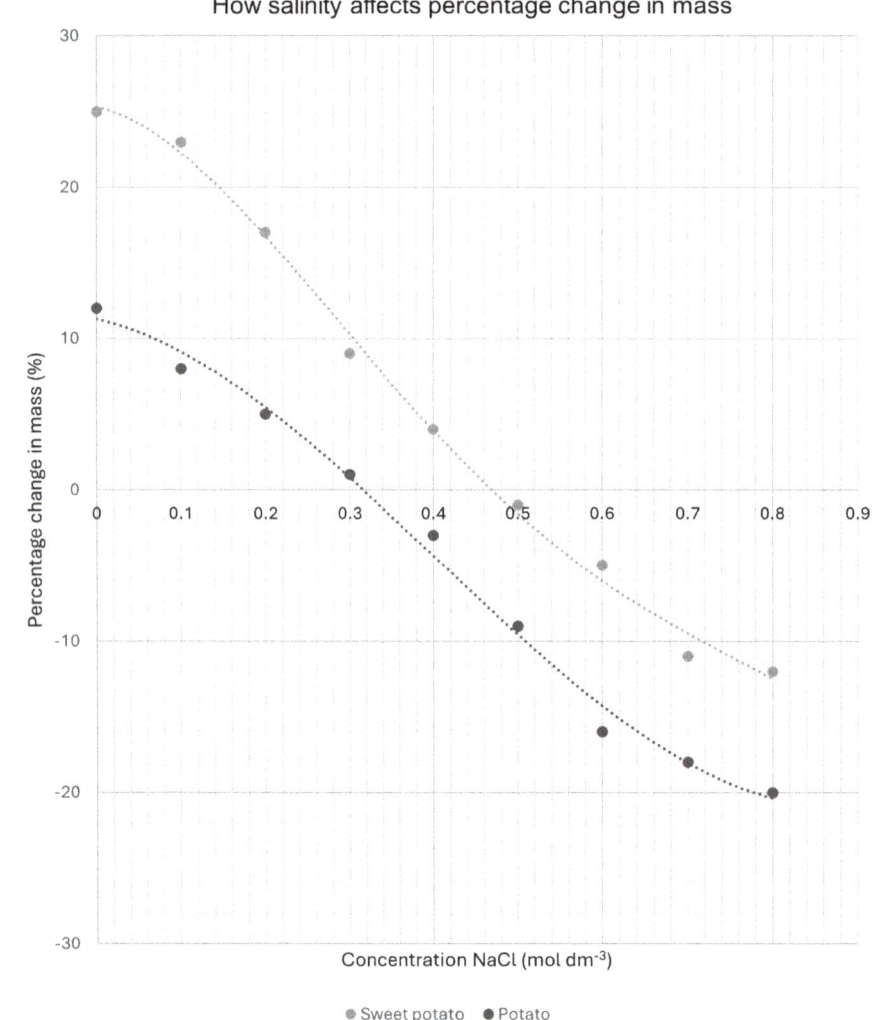

(a) State a controlled variable in the experiment. **[1]**

....

(b) Determine the isotonic point of potato and sweet potato. **[2]**

....

ANSWER ANALYSIS

A controlled variable is a variable that is kept constant for a fair test. Examiners are looking for variables that should be controlled and are not explicitly mentioned in the question.

The isotonic point is where the potato neither gained or lost mass.

Water moves from a hypotonic (dilute solution) to a hypertonic (concentrated solution). Osmosis is the movement of water from a dilute to a concentrated solution across a partially permeable membrane. If the tissue gains water by osmosis the solution is hypotonic (dilute), if the tissue loses water by osmosis the solution is hypertonic (concentrated).

(c) Suggest a concentration where the potato is in a hypertonic solution and the sweet potato is in a hypotonic solution. [1]

(d) Identify two sources of error in the procedure. [2]

Below is the nutritional information for potatoes and sweet potatoes.

Nutrient per 100 g	Potatoes	Sweet potatoes
Water (g)	79	77
Energy (kJ)	322	360
Protein (g)	2.0	1.6
Fat (g)	0.09	0.05
Carbohydrates (g)	17	20
Fibre (g)	2.2	3
Sugar (g)	0.78	4.18

(e) Deduce the reason for the difference in the isotonic point between potato and sweet potato. [1]

2. A student investigated the effect of temperature on the rate of respiration of maggots using the respirometer below. The student observed that the maggots wriggled more as the temperature increased from 20°C to 30°C.

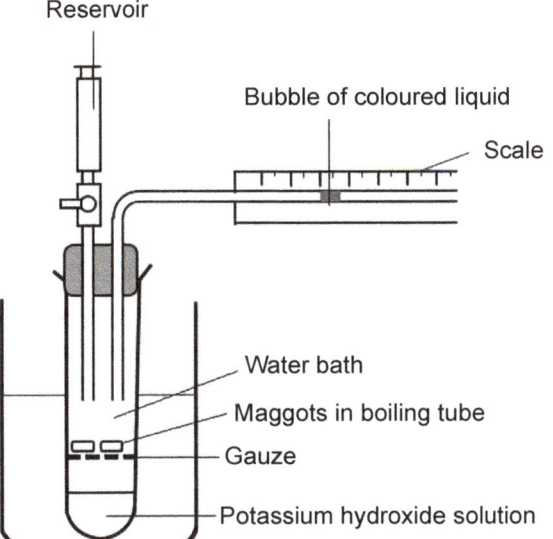

(a) Outline **one** factor that ensures the maggots are not harmed. [1]

(b) Before recording any data, the student left the experiment for 10 minutes. Suggest why this improved the validity of the experiment. [1]

....

....

The graph below shows the distance the bubble moved in three temperatures.

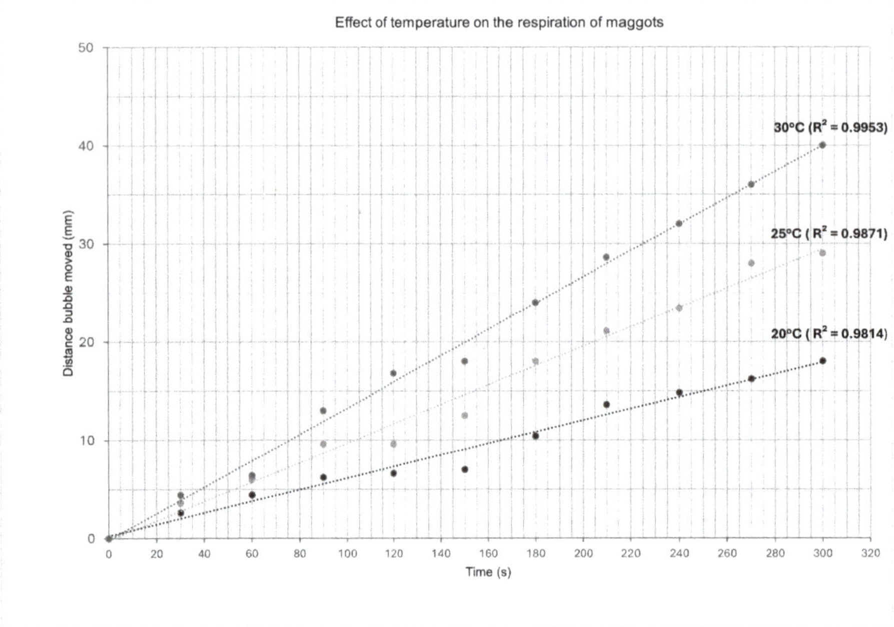

Effect of temperature on the respiration of maggots

[Graph showing distance bubble moved (mm) vs Time (s), with three lines: 30°C ($R^2 = 0.9953$), 25°C ($R^2 = 0.9871$), 20°C ($R^2 = 0.9814$)]

(c) Calculate the rate of respiration in mm^3 per minute for the maggots at 30°C. [1]

....

(d) Deduce the effect of temperature on the rate of aerobic respiration shown in the graph. [1]

....

....

(e) Explain why the bubble of coloured liquid moves during the experiment. [2]

....

....

....

....

(f) Suggest an improvement to the quality of data in the experiment. [1]

....

....

3. The image below shows a scanning electron micrograph of a stoma in a tomato leaf

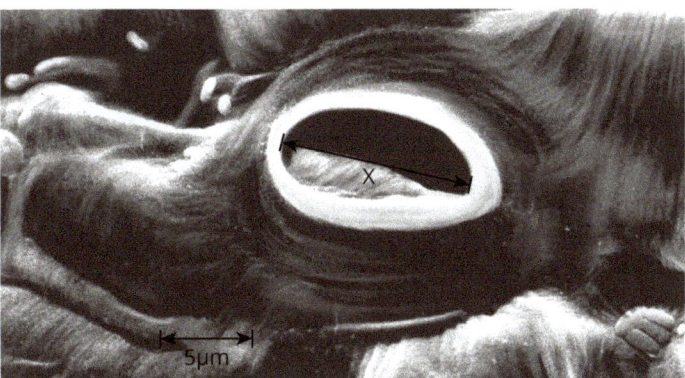

  Magnification = image size / actual size.

Use a ruler to measure the scale bar length in mm.

Check all units are in μm
1 mm = 1000 μm

Use scale bar to calculate magnification first. Then measure image size of pore in mm and convert to μm.

(a) Calculate the diameter of the stomatal pore indicated by X. [1]

(b) Outline the role of stomata when open and closed. [2]

(c) Draw a plan diagram, with labels, to show the distribution of tissues in a transverse section of a dicotyledonous leaf. [3]

4. The table below shows the genus of coral found at different depths at the Marine Park in Sulaweisi, Indonesia, Kaledupa.

Genus of coral	5 m depth		10 m depth	
	n	n(n – 1)	n	n(n – 1)
Acropora	15	210	25	600
Astreopora	3	6	12	132
Cyphastrea	0	0	3	6
Diploastrea	0	0	3	6
Euphyllia	4	12	1	0
Favia	14	182	10	90
Favites	8	56	12	132
Fungia	15	210	6	30
Galaxea	4	12	4	12
Goniapora	2	2	2	2
Goniasrea	24	552	26	650
Heliofungia	1	0	1	0
Leptoseris	3	6	16	240
Montipora	5	20	8	56
Mycedium	0	0	2	2
Pachyseris	0	0	0	0
Physogyra	0	0	4	12
Plerogyra	4	12	10	90
Pocillopora	8	56	17	272
Porites	45	1980	31	930
Sarcophyton	33	1056	23	506
Seriatopora	4	12	16	240
Stylophora	18	306	27	702
Symphyllia	9	72	3	6
Turbinaria	0	0	2	2
Total	**219**	**4762**	**264**	**4718**
Simpson's reciprocal index		**10.03**		

[Source: Adapted from Table 2: David J. Smith, 'Marine Report: Marine biodiversity and ecology of the Wakatobi Marine National Park', *Southeast Sulawesi* (August 2003) p.62 (https://cdn.yello.link/opwall/files/2017/11/Opwall-Indonesia-Wakatobi-Marine-Science-Report-2003.pdf)]

(a) One way of measuring diversity is species richness. State the species richness for 5 m and 10 m. [2]

5 m: .... 10 m: ....

Species richness refers to how many different species are present.

Simpson's reciprocal diversity index, D, is a more accurate method used to calculate the diversity of an ecosystem as it takes into account both species richness and evenness.

(b) Distinguish between the terms richness and evenness. [2]

....

....

Learn definitions. Species evenness is the relative abundance of each species.

(c) Use the formula below and the totals in the table to calculate Simpson's reciprocal index for 10 m. [1]

$$D = \frac{N(N-1)}{\sum n(n-1)}$$

N = total number of individuals.
n = number of individuals of a species.

....

....

Set B

Paper 2: Standard Level

Set your timer for **1 hour and 30 minutes**

- The maximum mark for this examination paper is **[50 marks]**
- **Section A** - answer ALL the questions
- **Section B** - answer **one** question
- A calculator is needed for this paper

Section A

1. A study in Hawaii has investigated how carbon dioxide emissions affect the ocean. Atmospheric CO_2 has been monitored since 1958 in Mauna Loa. Seawater carbon dioxide levels (measured as partial pressure pCO_2) and pH have been monitored at station ALOHA, which is north of Hawaii.

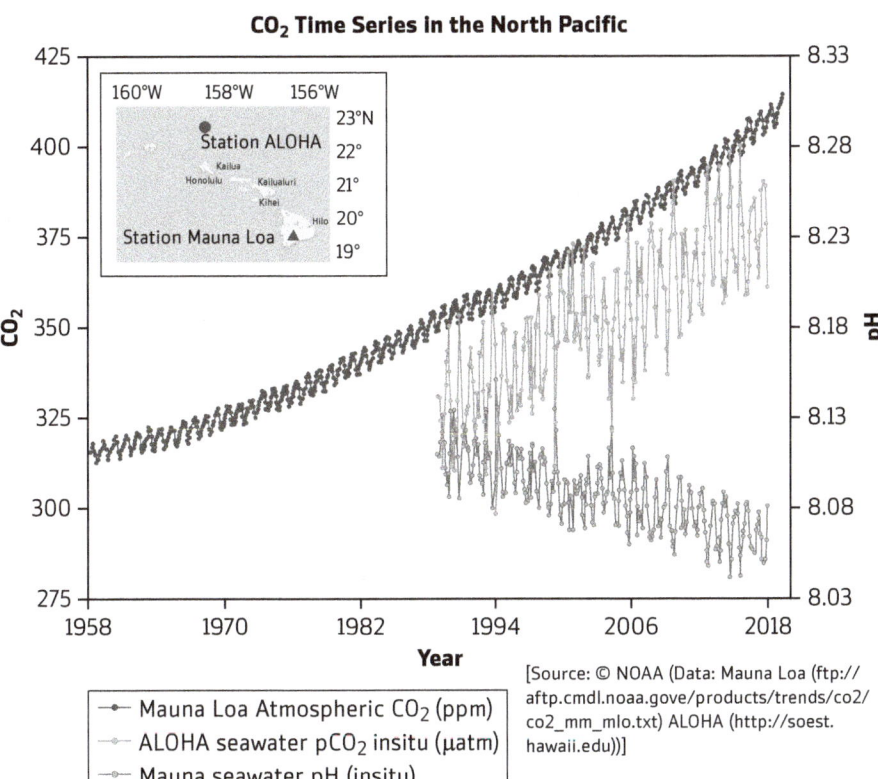

[Source: © NOAA (Data: Mauna Loa (ftp://aftp.cmdl.noaa.gove/products/trends/co2/co2_mm_mlo.txt) ALOHA (http://soest.hawaii.edu))]

(a) State the year ALOHA started measuring pCO_2 and pH of seawater. **[1]**

....

....

(b) Calculate the percentage increase in atmospheric CO_2 concentration between 1958 and 2018. **[1]**

....

> **Greenhouse gases** such as methane and carbon dioxide absorb the infrared radiation (heat) and re-radiate the heat. The more greenhouse gases present, the more heat is re-radiated and the hotter the atmosphere becomes.

> Use a ruler to draw down from the graph and read accurately off the X-axis. Each division is 12 years.

> ! Check you are looking at the correct line and axis.

> Percentage change = (change/original) × 100%
> = (412−316)/316 × 100%

> **ANSWER ANALYSIS**
> To calculate this answer, you should draw a vertical line down from where the measurements first appear.
> 1958 = 316 ppm (315–320 ppm)
> 2018 = 412 ppm (410–415 ppm)

(c) Describe the evidence that shows the atmospheric CO_2 affects the seawater pCO_2 and pH. [2]

....

....

....

....

> **DESCRIBE**
> Describe requires a detailed account.

> Look at the graph and the trend. It helps to say "as (name of X-axis) increases, (name of Y-axis) increases or decreases". The question here wants the trend for both pCO_2 and pH. Sometimes the graph may reach a peak or plateau – it doesn't in this example. Often it helps if there are error bars to comment on the variation in the data. Here there are no error bars but there is a repeating trend. It may also be worth commenting that the correlation is not a causation.

(d) Outline three causes of increased carbon dioxide in oceans. [3]

....

....

....

....

....

....

> To answer this you need to outline factors that are leading to increased carbon dioxide concentrations in the atmosphere and how this carbon dioxide reaches the ocean.

Acidification of oceans is a threat to the marine organisms such as the Antarctic pteropod *Limacina helicina*. Pteropods are a type of zooplankton with a calcium carbonate shell. They are rich in fatty acids and are eaten by krill, whales and North Pacific juvenile salmon. A study was carried out in which a pteropod shell was placed in seawater with the predicted pH (7.8) and carbonate levels projected for 2100. The photos below show the shell transparency over 45 days.

| 0 days | 15 days | 30 days | 45 days |

(e) Identify what domain the pteropod belongs to. [1]

....

> There are three domains: Bacteria, Archaea and Eukaryota.

The study below shows the percentage mortality of *Limacina helicina* after 29 days of incubation at different water temperatures and pCO₂ concentrations.

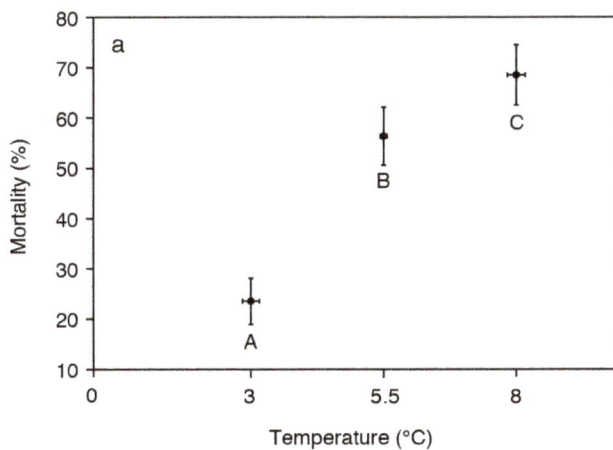

[Source: S. Lischka, J. Budenbender, T. Boxhammer, and U. Riebesell, 'Impact of ocean acidification and elevated temperatures on early juveniles of the polar shelled pteropod *Limacina helicina*: mortality, shell degradation, and shell growth' (*Biogeosciences*, 15 April 2011, CC BY 3.0)]

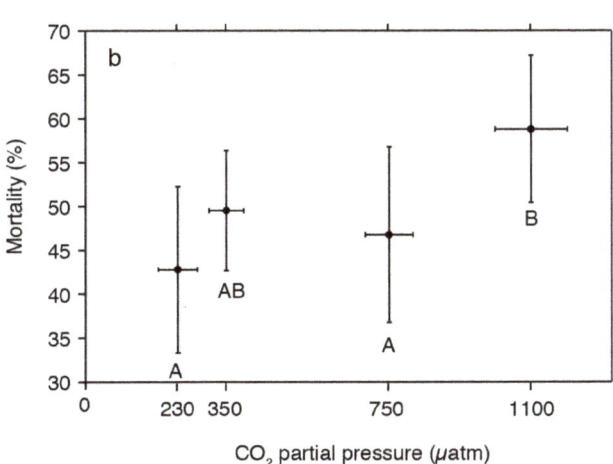

(f) Describe the trend in mortality when temperature is increased. **[2]**

Check you are looking at the top graph for temperature.

(g) Explain reasons for the change in the shell of *Limacina helicina* over the 45 days. **[3]**

ANSWER ANALYSIS

The explain question requires a detailed account of the reasons/causes linking acidity to the damage in calcium carbonate shells.

(h) Suggest the effect of increased carbon dioxide
    concentrations on salmon populations. [2]

....

....

....

....

2. (a) Label the parts of the DNA molecule indicated by I, II, III, IV. [2]

I ....   III ....

II ....   IV ....

(b) Outline the following terms in relation to the genetic code.
    (i) Degenerate .... [1]

    ....

    (ii) Universal .... [1]

    ....

(c) Distinguish between eukaryotic and prokaryotic DNA. [2]

....

....

....

....

(d) Outline the role of two enzymes in DNA replication. [2]

....

....

....

....

3. The image shows a cross-section through a coronavirus which is responsible for many respiratory issues such as colds, Flu and COVID-19. It consists of a protein coat and RNA.

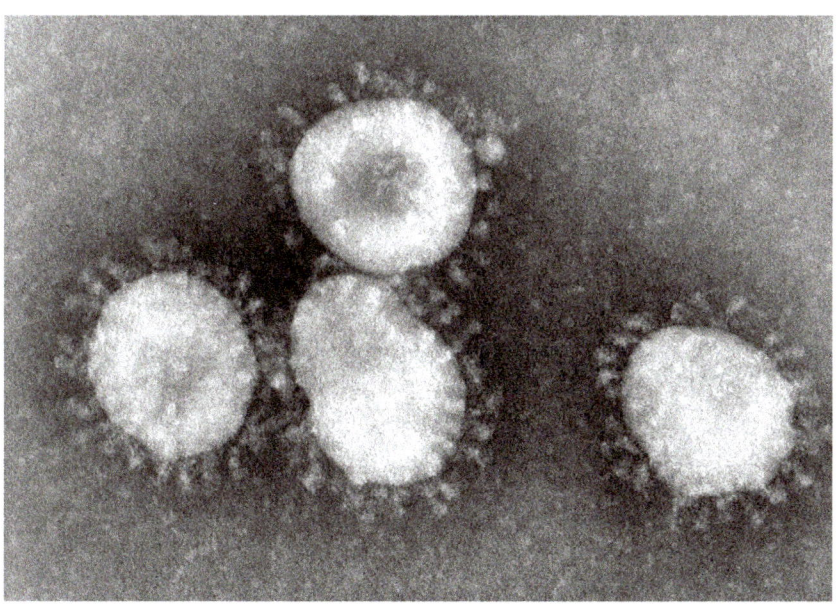

(a) State, with a reason, the type of microscope used to produce the image. **[1]**

> Viruses are smaller than bacteria. Bacteria cannot be seen with a light microscope. The term cross-section should also give you a clue.

(b) State two reasons viruses are not considered to be living. **[2]**

(c) Outline why antibiotics would not be effective in treating people infected with coronaviruses. **[2]**

> You need to explain why antibiotics do not work on viruses.

4. Below is an image of an artery and vein taken with a light microscope x 100.

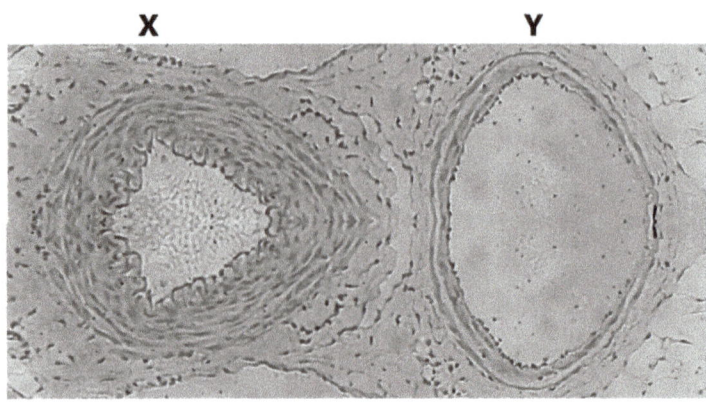

X   Y

(a) Justify which image is an artery. [2]

(b) Outline how arteries are adapted to transport blood away from the heart. [2]

(c) Suggest two methods to find the pulse rate (beats per minute). [2]

JUSTIFY

Justify means give valid reasons or evidence to support an answer or conclusion.

Section B

Answer **one** question from a choice of two.

5. Approximately 71 percent of the earth's surface is covered in water. Water is essential for life, influencing biological processes at molecular, organismal, and environmental levels.

    (a) Describe how changes in weather conditions affect the transport and loss of water in terrestrial plants. **[5]**

    > Water is transported in the xylem and is lost through transpiration. What weather conditions can affect transpiration rates?

    (b) Outline the formation of a dipeptide. **[3]**

    > Draw the formation of a dipeptide, or explain which groups bond with which.

    > A dipeptide is made up of two amino acids. Show their structure in your drawing.

    > What process takes place when joining two monomers together?

> What is the name of the bond forming between the two amino acids?

! Don't forget to include the role of water in the process!

(c) Explain the physical properties of water and the consequences for animals in aquatic arctic habitats [7]

> Water is polar. Link to structure of water then properties and real-life examples, e.g. high latent heat of vaporization and high specific heat capacity. Remember the differences between thermal conductivity, high latent heat of vaporization and high specific heat capacity.

ANSWER ANALYSIS

Up to one additional mark is available for the construction of your answers for each question.

> What type of bonds form between the polar water molecules?

> How are these bonds related to the specific properties of water?

> Outlining the properties of water is not enough. Each property must be linked to its significance in organisms.

6. The genes on human chromosomes 2 and 12 demonstrate how genetic features influence immunity, circadian rhythms, and evolutionary history in humans. Chromosome 2 plays a major role in immune and inflammatory responses, while chromosome 12 contains the CRY gene, which regulates the circadian rhythm.

(a) Explain the production of antibodies in humans, highlighting their role in the immune response. [5]

> Which cells are responsible for producing specific antibodies against foreign antigens? How are these cells activated?

(b) Outline the role of melatonin in the regulation of the sleep-wake cycle. [3]

(c) Evaluate the evidence supporting the hypothesis that chromosome 2 in humans arose from the fusion of chromosomes 12 and 13 with a shared primate ancestor. [7]

Set C

This set of papers has no additional help in the margins. There is a space to write notes so you can plan what you are going to write if needed.

Paper 1A: Standard Level

- Set your timer for 1 hour 30 minutes [**Paper 1A and Paper 1B**].
- Each question is worth [**1**] mark.
- For each question, choose the answer you consider to be the best and put a tick next to it in the book.
- A calculator is required for this paper.
- The maximum mark for paper 1A is [**30 marks**].

NOTES

1. Which of these statements explains the polarity of water? [1]

   ☐ A. The oxygen in one water molecule has a slight negative charge that covalently bonds with the slight positive charge of the hydrogen from another water molecule

   ☐ B. The oxygen in one water molecule has a slight positive charge that covalently bonds with the slight negative charge of hydrogen from another water molecule

   ☐ C. The oxygen in one water molecule has a slight negative charge that forms hydrogen bonds with the slight positive charge of the hydrogen from another water molecule

   ☐ D. The oxygen in one water molecule has a slight positive charge that forms hydrogen bonds with the slight negative charge of hydrogen from another water molecule

2. The percentage of adenine in the DNA of an organism is approximately 30%. What is the percentage of guanine? [1]

   ☐ A. 70%

   ☐ B. 30%

   ☐ C. 40%

   ☐ D. 20%

3. The diagram below shows a molecule. Identify the correct name of the molecule and the parts labelled X, Y and Z. [1]

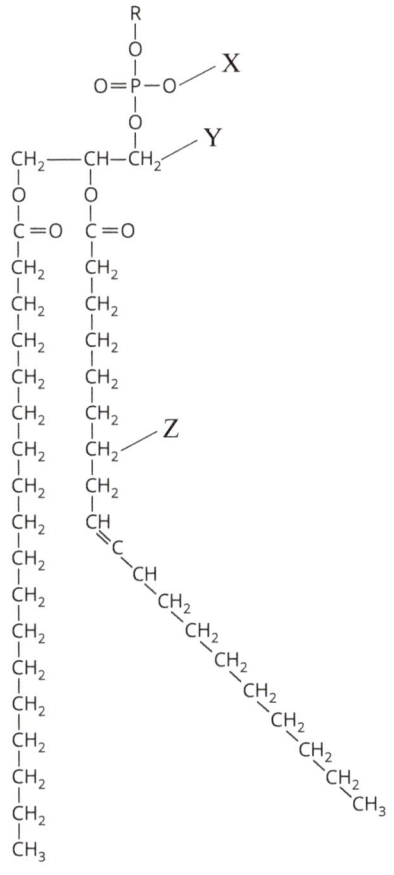

	Molecule name	X	Y	Z
☐ A.	Phospholipid	Glycerol	Protein	Fatty acid tail
☐ B.	Phospholipid	Phosphate	Glycerol	Fatty acid tail
☐ C.	Glycoprotein	Glycerol	Glycerol	Amino acid tail
☐ D.	Glycoprotein	Phosphate	Protein	Amino acid tail

4. The diagram below shows two molecules. Identify the correct name of the molecules. [1]

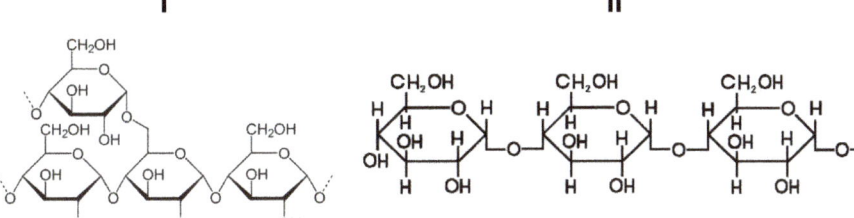

	I	II
☐ A.	α-glucose	Cellulose
☐ B.	Cellulose	β-glucose
☐ C.	Amylose	Amylopectin
☐ D.	Amylopectin	Amylose

5. Which of these graphs shows the effect of pH on enzyme activity?
[1]

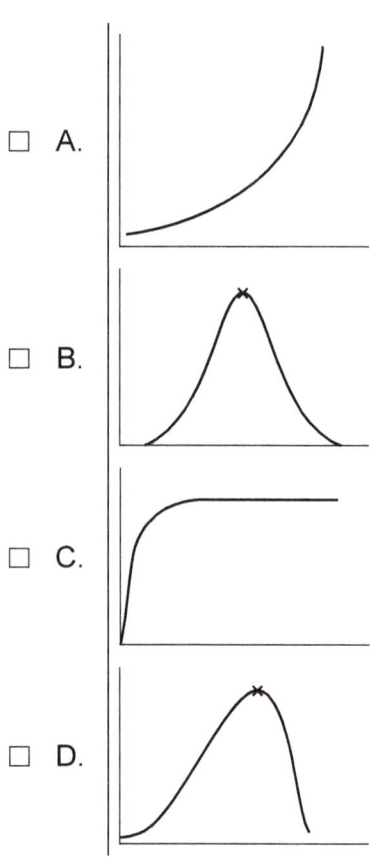

☐ A.

☐ B.

☐ C.

☐ D.

6. The experiment below was set up to look at the effect of respiration and photosynthesis. Bromothymol blue is:

- blue when CO_2 is low (pH 8)
- green at pH 7
- yellow when CO_2 is high (pH 6).

Four test tubes were set up to investigate photosynthesis and respiration.

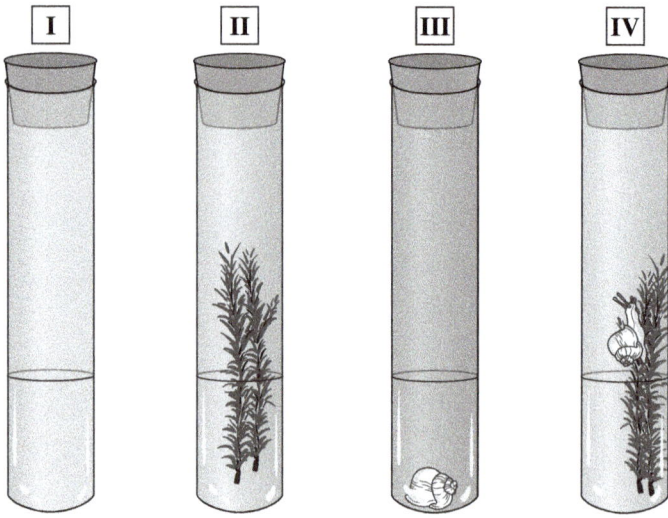

I: Control: no living organisms
II: Plant only
III: Pond snails only
IV: Pond snails and pondweed

- Test tube I is a control and stayed green.
- Test tube II changed colour to blue.
- Test tube III changed colour to yellow.
- Test tube IV changed colour to blue.

What conclusion can be drawn from these results? [1]

	II	III	IV
☐ A.	Photosynthesis is faster than respiration	Only respiration is occurring	Photosynthesis is faster than respiration
☐ B.	Only photosynthesis is occurring	Only respiration is occurring	Both photosynthesis and respiration are occurring
☐ C.	Respiration is faster than photosynthesis	Photosynthesis is faster than respiration	Respiration is faster than photosynthesis
☐ D.	Only respiration is occurring	Only photosynthesis is occurring	Both photosynthesis and respiration are occurring

7. How are tiny amounts of DNA amplified? [1]

   ☐ A. Gel electrophoresis

   ☐ B. PCR

   ☐ C. DNA profiling

   ☐ D. Cloning

8. The antisense sequence of a short section of DNA is shown along with the mRNA that has been transcribed from it. Which are the possible mRNA codons that could be transcribed and what is the first tRNA anticodon that could translate the DNA? [1]

	DNA	mRNA codon	First possible tRNA anticodon
☐ A.	AUCGGCAAAGCA	ATCGGCAAAGCA	TAG
☐ B.	ATCGGCAAAGCA	UAGCCGUUUCGU	AUC
☐ C.	TAGCCGTTTGCA	UAGCCGUUUCGU	AUC
☐ D.	UAGCCGUUUCGU	ATCGGATTTGCA	TAG

9. Which enzyme is used in transcription but not translation? [1]

   ☐ A. DNA helicase

   ☐ B. RNA polymerase

   ☐ C. DNA ligase

   ☐ D. Reverse transcriptase

10. What is the proteome of a species? [1]

    ☐ A. The entire set of proteins that can be expressed by an organism
    ☐ B. The total amount of DNA that can be transcribed by an organism
    ☐ C. The name of the bond that forms between two amino acids
    ☐ D. A chain of amino acids joined by condensation reactions

11. Which are features of tRNA?

    I. Triplet of bases called an anticodon
    II. Attachment site for amino acids
    III. A pairs with T and C pairs with G by complementary base pairing [1]

    ☐ A. I only
    ☐ B. I and II only
    ☐ C. II and III only
    ☐ D. I, II and III

12. In 1986 the Chernobyl nuclear accident sent out a large amount of the radioactive isotope of iodine into the environment.

    The graph below shows the number of cases of thyroid cancer per 100,000 people in the following years.

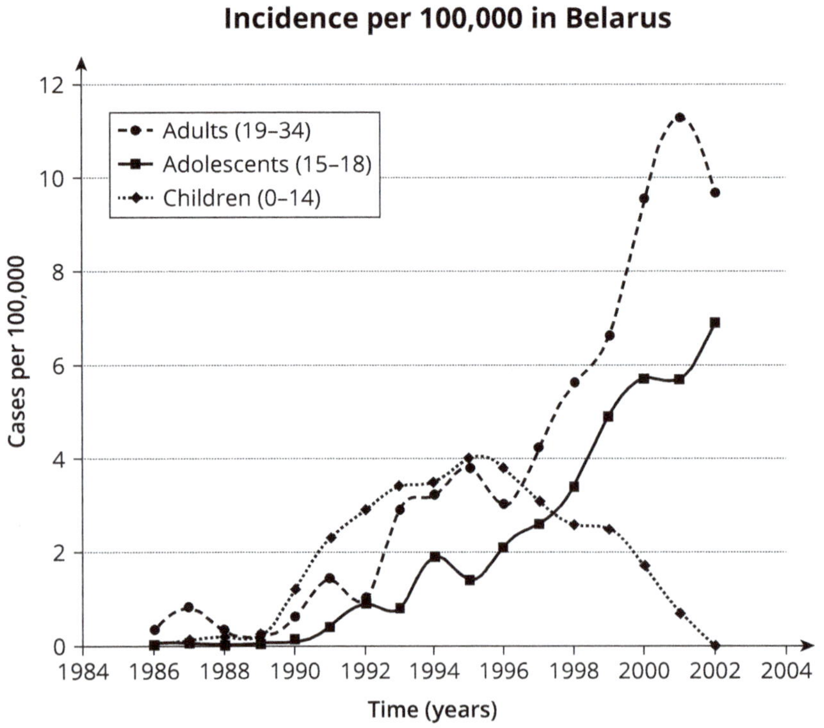

    Incidence per 100,000 in Belarus

    [Graph showing cases per 100,000 vs Time (years) from 1984 to 2004, with three lines for Adults (19–34), Adolescents (15–18), and Children (0–14)]

    What conclusions can be made from this graph? [1]

    ☐ A. Adults had the greatest exposure to iodine ^{131}I
    ☐ B. All the children affected died by 2002
    ☐ C. A higher number of adults developed cancer than any other age group
    ☐ D. Chernobyl caused all the cases of cancer

13. The electron micrograph below shows a eukaryotic organelle.

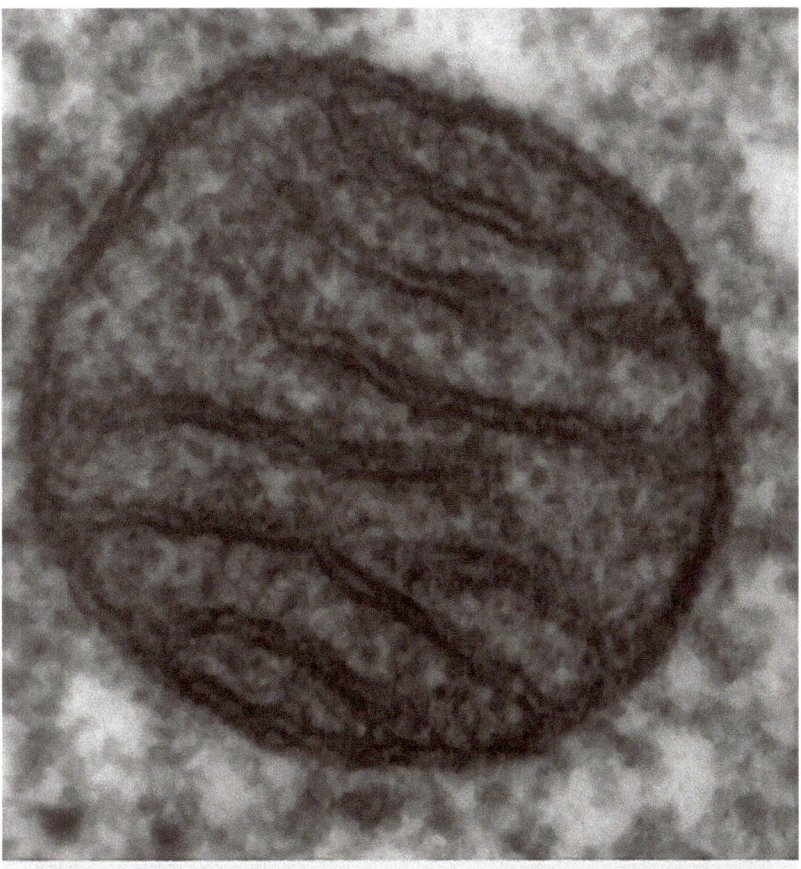

50 nm   08LungTEM

What is the magnification of the image? [1]

☐ A. × 8000

☐ B. × 80000

☐ C. × 800000

☐ D. × 8000000

14. A cell has cytoplasm, a cell wall, a nucleoid and 70S ribosomes. Based on this information, what type of cell could this be? [1]

☐ A. A yeast

☐ B. A cell from an oak tree

☐ C. A bacterium

☐ D. A human skin cell

15. Which statement about surface area to volume ratio is true? [1]

☐ A. As cells increase in size their surface area to volume ratio increases

☐ B. Smaller cells have a higher surface area to volume ratio than larger cells

☐ C. A small surface area to volume ratio is needed to allow fast diffusion of oxygen into cells

☐ D. A small surface area to volume ratio releases less heat

16. Which of the following is **not** a feature of stem cells? [1]

☐ A. They have the ability to specialize

☐ B. They are differentiated

☐ C. They can be obtained from embryos

☐ D. They divide by mitosis to provide many cells

17. Which part of the motor neuron below is correctly matched to its name and function? [1]

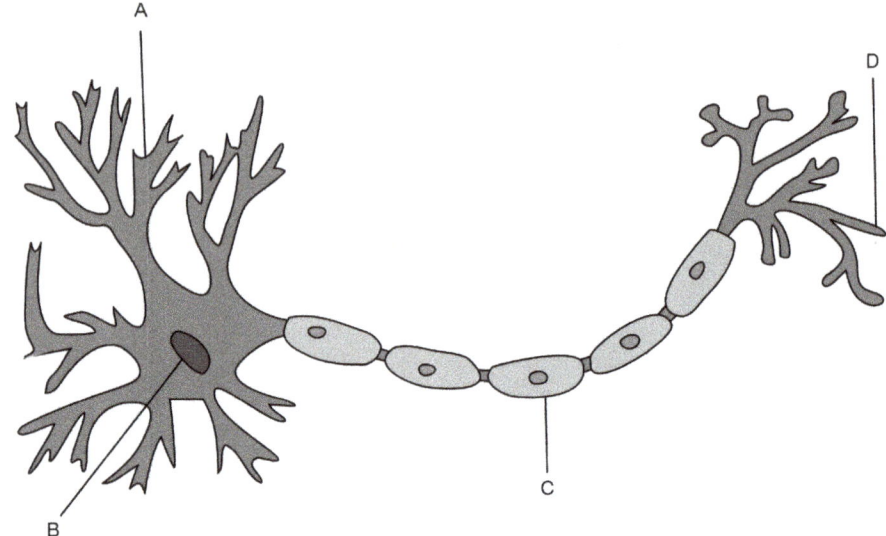

	Name	Function
☐ A.	Dendrites	Sends neurotransmitter to muscle cell
☐ B.	Nucleus	Initiates action potential
☐ C.	Myelin sheath	Speeds up transmission of nerve impulse
☐ D.	Presynaptic knob	Initiates action potential

18. Which mitotic phase corresponds to the labels in the micrograph of an onion (*Allium cepa*)? [1]

	I	II	III
☐ A.	Anaphase	Telophase	Prophase
☐ B.	Metaphase	Prophase	Telophase
☐ C.	Prophase	Metaphase	Anaphase
☐ D.	Telophase	Anaphase	Metaphase

19. The four images show different stages of cell division in a cell. What type of cells could be dividing? [1]

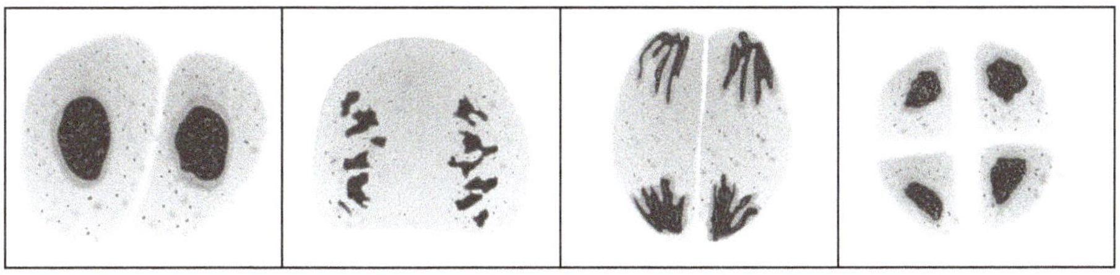

☐ A. Bacterial cells during asexual reproduction

☐ B. Red blood cells in bone marrow

☐ C. Skin cells regenerating cells lost

☐ D. Cells in the testes to produce sperm cells

20. The dog vomit slime mould *Fuligo septica* belongs to what genus? [1]

☐ A. Animalia

☐ B. Fungi

☐ C. *Fuligo*

☐ D. *F. septica*

21. What is the function of the hormone melatonin? [1]

☐ A. Control of appetite

☐ B. Control of heart rate

☐ C. Control of circadian rhythms

☐ D. Control of menstrual cycle

22. What is the name of the insoluble protein that forms a mesh of fibres in a blood clot? **[1]**

- ☐ A. Fibrinogen
- ☐ B. Fibrin
- ☐ C. Prothrombin
- ☐ D. Thrombin

23. Below is an image of the male reproductive system. What are the correct labels for I, II and III? **[1]**

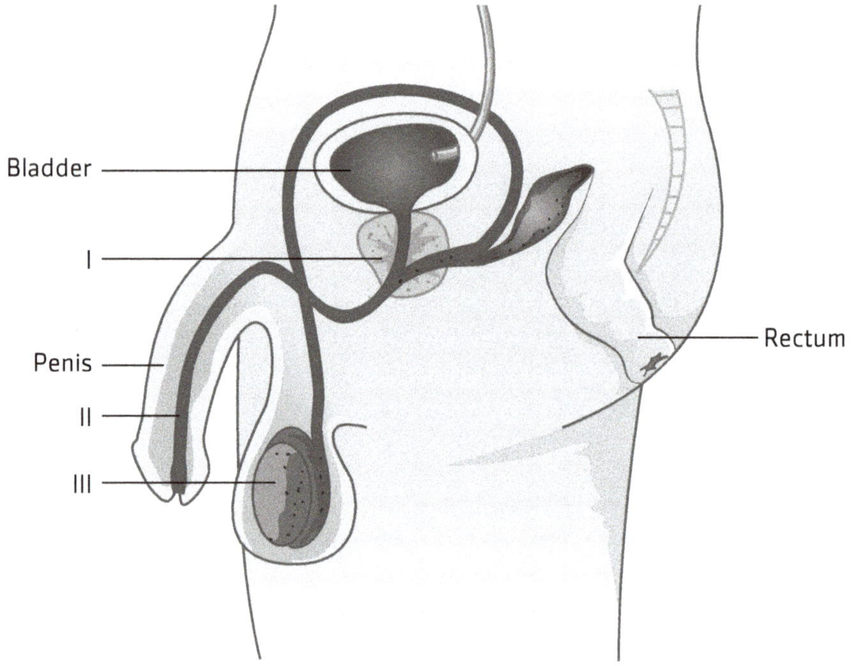

	I	II	III
☐ A.	Epididymis	Ureter	Testicle
☐ B.	Prostate gland	Urethra	Testis
☐ C.	Epididymis	Urethra	Testicle
☐ D.	Prostate gland	Ureter	Testis

24. Which of the following are not true about the male gamete? **[1]**

- ☐ A. The male gamete travels towards the female gamete
- ☐ B. The size of the male gamete is smaller in comparison to the female gamete
- ☐ C. The male gamete carries more food reserves than the female gamete
- ☐ D. There are often many more male gametes produced than female gametes

25. The following diagram shows the human menstrual cycle.

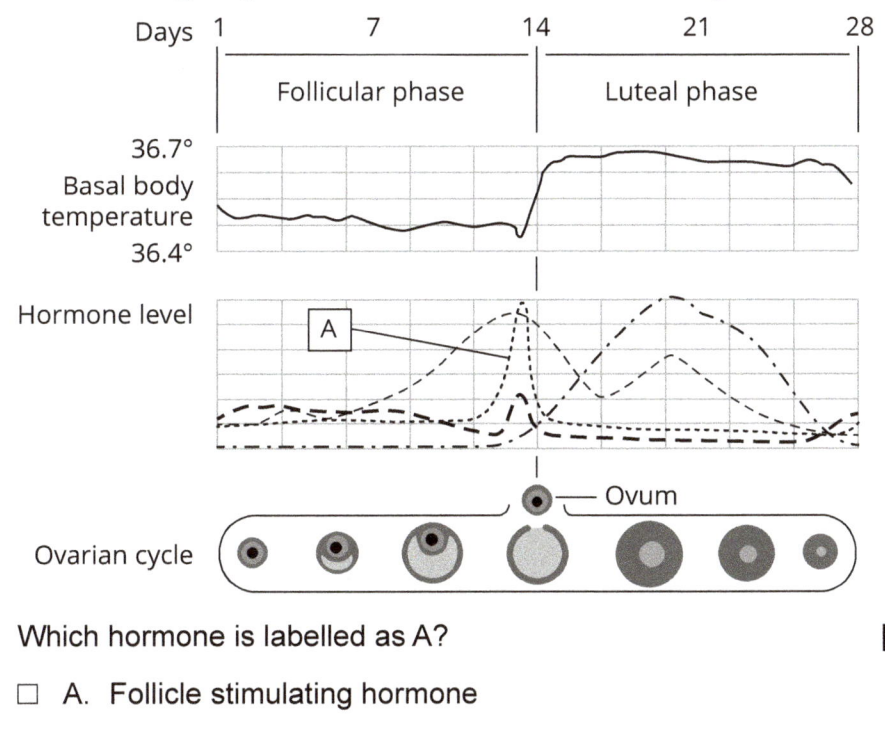

Which hormone is labelled as A? [1]

☐ A. Follicle stimulating hormone

☐ B. Luteinizing hormone

☐ C. Oestrogen

☐ D. Progesterone

26. A parent organism with an unknown genotype is mated in a test cross. Approximately 50% of the offspring have the same phenotype as the unknown parent. What can be concluded? [1]

☐ A. The unknown parent is homozygous recessive for the trait

☐ B. The unknown parent is homozygous dominant for the trait

☐ C. The unknown parent is heterozygous for the trait

☐ D. The unknown parent is co-dominant for the trait

27. Which hormone is released from which tissue in the pancreas if blood sugar levels are too low? [1]

☐ A. Glucagon is released by alpha cells in the islets of Langerhans

☐ B. Insulin is released by beta cells in the islets of Langerhans

☐ C. Glucagon is released by beta cells in the islets of Langerhans

☐ D. Insulin is released by alpha cells in the islets of Langerhans

28. Which organism is correctly matched with its mode of nutrition? **[1]**

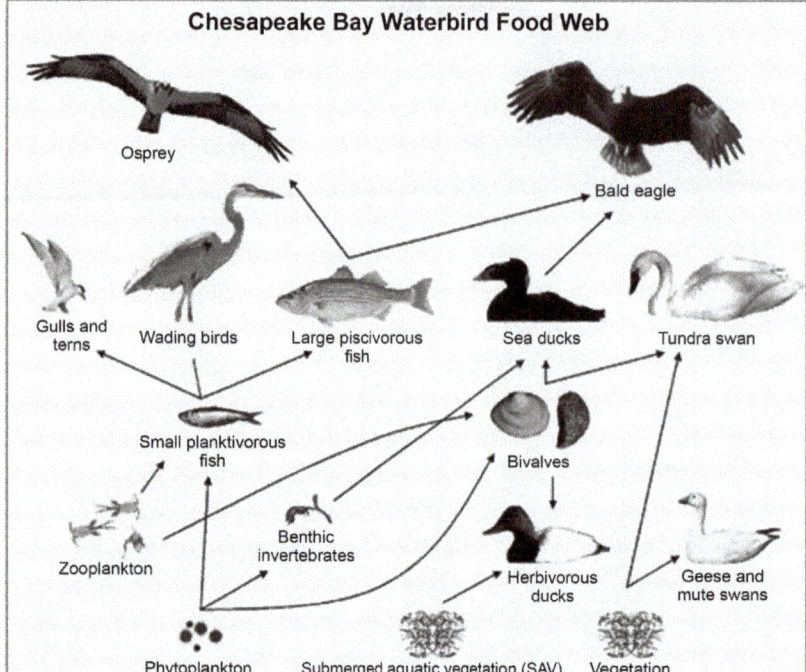

- ☐ A. An osprey is prey to the bald eagle
- ☐ B. Phytoplankton are herbivores
- ☐ C. The bald eagle is a tertiary consumer
- ☐ D. The large piscivorous fish is prey to the sea ducks

29. What is the correct definition of a community? **[1]**

- ☐ A. A group of organisms of the same species, living in the same geographical area at the same time
- ☐ B. A group of populations living together and interacting with each other within a given area at the same time
- ☐ C. The environment in which a species lives
- ☐ D. A group of populations interacting with each other and their abiotic environment

30. Below is a diagram of the carbon cycle.

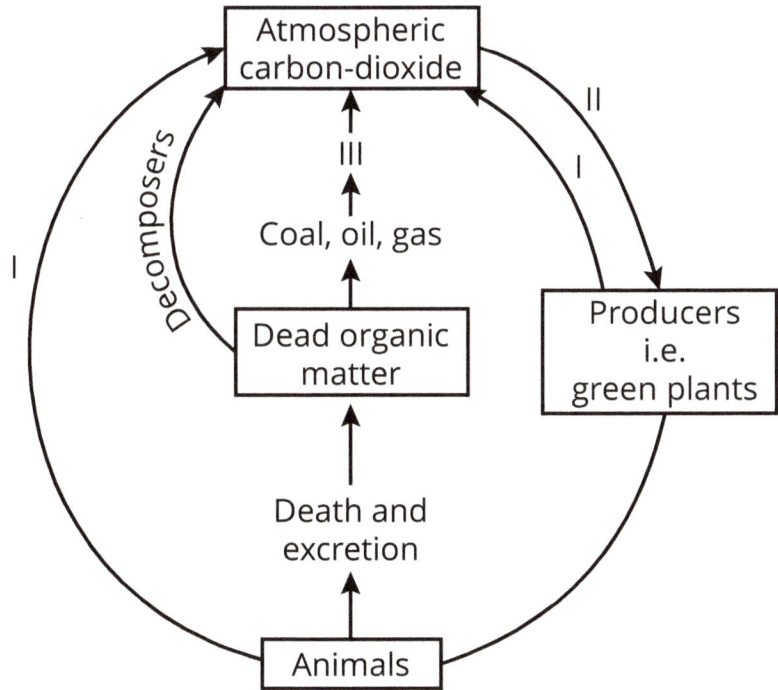

What do processes I, II and III represent? [1]

	I	II	III
☐ A.	Respiration	Photosynthesis	Fossilization
☐ B.	Respiration	Photosynthesis	Combustion
☐ C.	Photosynthesis	Respiration	Combustion
☐ D.	Photosynthesis	Respiration	Fossilization

Set C

Paper 1B: Standard Level

- Answer all the questions.
- Answers must be written on the answer lines provided. Continue on another piece of paper if you need to.
- A calculator is required for this paper.
- The maximum mark for paper 1B is **[25 marks]**.

1. Bluebells *Hyacinthoides non-scripta* and wild garlic *Allium ursinum* are species often found in the same ancient woodland where they compete for resources.

Hyacinthoides non-scripta   *Allium ursinum*

   (a) Define species. **[1]**

   ....

   ....

   (b) Suggest a resource that *Hyacinthoides non-scripta* and *Allium ursinum* compete for. **[1]**

   ....

   ....

   A student investigated if there is an association between bluebells and wild garlic by testing the presence or absence of each species in 100 quadrats. Their contingency table is below.

	Bluebells present	**Bluebells absent**	Row totals
Wild garlic present	11	36	47
Wild garlic absent	48	5	53
Column totals	59	41	100

(c) Outline the method used to position the quadrats. [2]

....

....

....

....

A table of critical values is below.

df	0.995	0.99	0.975	0.95	0.90	0.10	0.05	0.025	0.01	0.005
1	...	...	0.001	0.004	0.016	2.706	3.841	5.024	6.635	7.879
2	0.010	0.020	0.051	0.103	0.211	4.605	5.991	7.378	9.210	10.597
3	0.072	0.115	0.216	0.352	0.584	6.251	7.815	9.348	11.345	12.838

(d) Use a suitable statistical test to determine if there is an association between the species. [4]

....

....

2. The image below is a light micrograph of broad bean (*Vicia faba*) root cells.

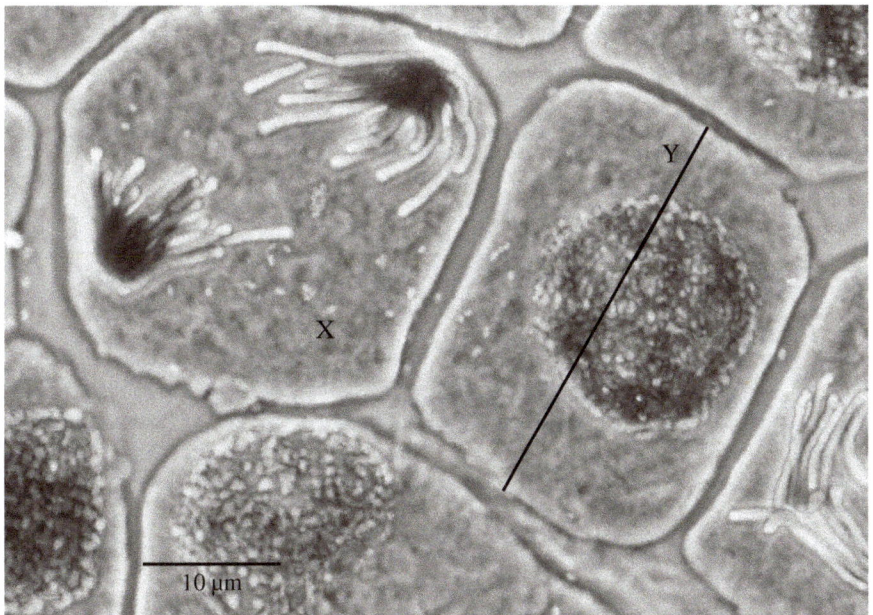

(a) Identify the stage of mitosis for cell X. [1]

....

(b) Calculate the magnification of the image. [1]

(c) Determine the actual length of cell Y. [1]

(d) Outline the effect of placing these cells in distilled water. [2]

3. A study investigated how the level of cholesterol in the blood affected death rate from coronary heart disease (CHD) in middle aged men in different populations.

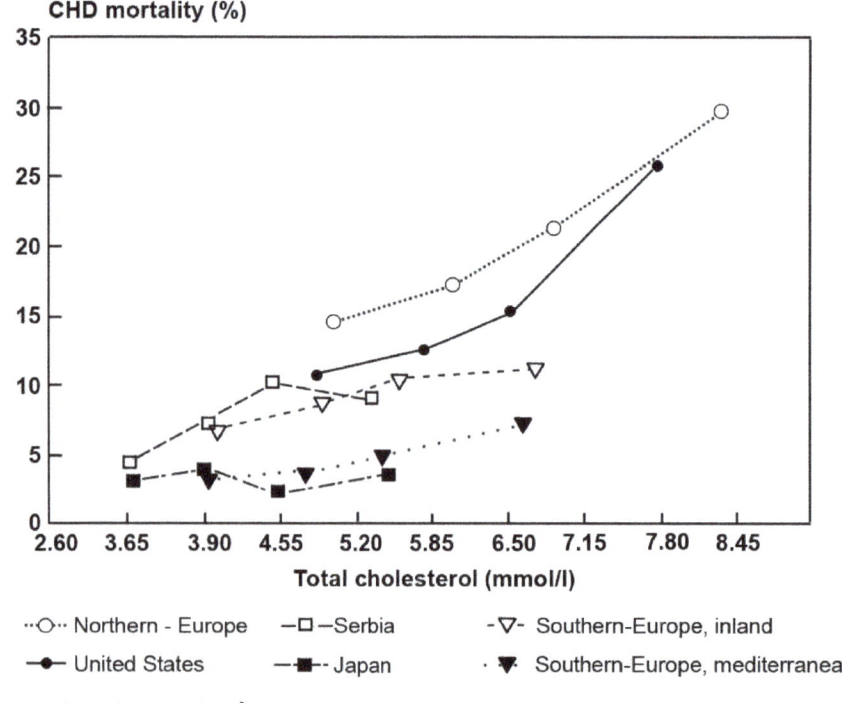

[Source: Seven Countries Study]

(a) State the overall trend between cholesterol and CHD mortality. [1]

(b) Identify the area whose population is most at risk of CHD. [1]

(c) Compare and contrast the data for Southern Europe, inland and Southern Europe, mediterranean. **[2]**

....

....

....

....

(d) Suggest a reason for the differences in data in Southern Europe, inland and Southern Europe, mediterranean. **[1]**

....

....

(e) Evaluate this hypothesis: 'Cholesterol causes CHD'. **[2]**

....

....

....

....

....

....

....

4. The image below shows a karyogram from a human female with Edwards' syndrome.

(a) What evidence is shown in the karyogram that this female has Edwards' syndrome? **[1]**

....

....

(b) What is the name of the process that results in the development of this syndrome. **[1]**

....

(c) Outline the inheritance and treatment of Phenylketonuria. **[3]**

....

....

....

....

....

....

Set C

Paper 2: Standard Level

Set your timer for **1 hour and 30 minutes**

- The maximum mark for this examination paper is **[50 marks]**
- **Section A** - answer ALL the questions
- **Section B** - answer **one** question
- A calculator is needed for this paper

Section A

1. Coronaviruses are a family of viruses that cause a range of illnesses from the common cold to Middle East Respiratory syndrome (MERS-CoV) and Severe Acute Respiratory Syndrome (SARS-CoV) as well SARS-CoV-2, which caused the COVID pandemic in 2019/20. This image shows the method of transfer of the three coronaviruses to humans.

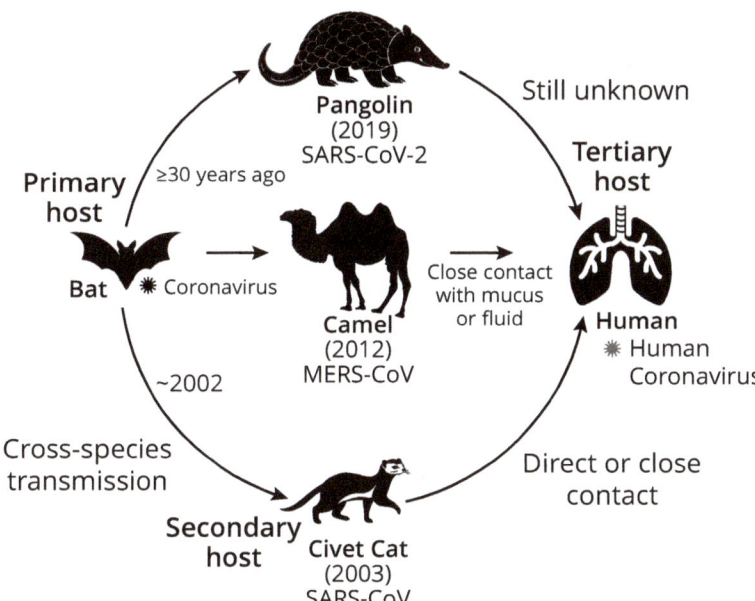

(a) State the name given to any disease that is transmitted between species from animals to humans. **[1]**

....

....

....

	Date	Countries affected	Cases	Deaths	Percentage deaths (%)
SARS-CoV	Nov 2002–July 2003	26.00	8097.00	774.00	9.56
MERS-CoV	2012	27.00	2494.00	858.00	34.40
SARS-CoV-2	2020–2024	229.00	776696616.00	7072509.00	

[Source: WHO. Figures from 3 November 2024]

(b) Calculate the percentage deaths from SARS-CoV-2 between 2020 and 2024. [1]

(c) Based on the data in the table, compare and contrast the severity of the three pandemics. [3]

The graphs show the epidemiological data for CoV-19 in China and Italy from 21 January 2020 to 11 March 2020.

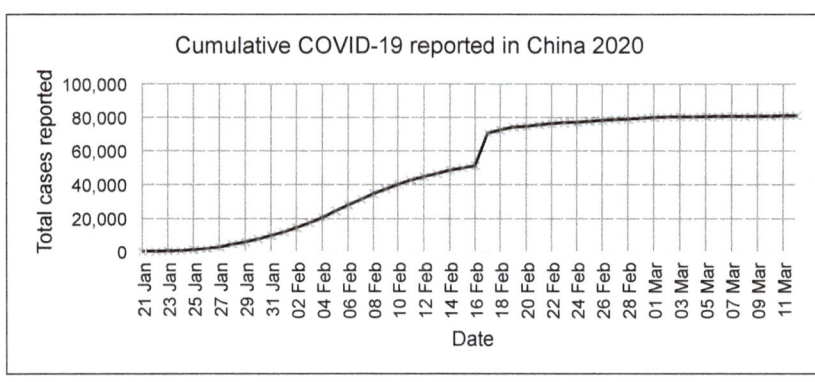

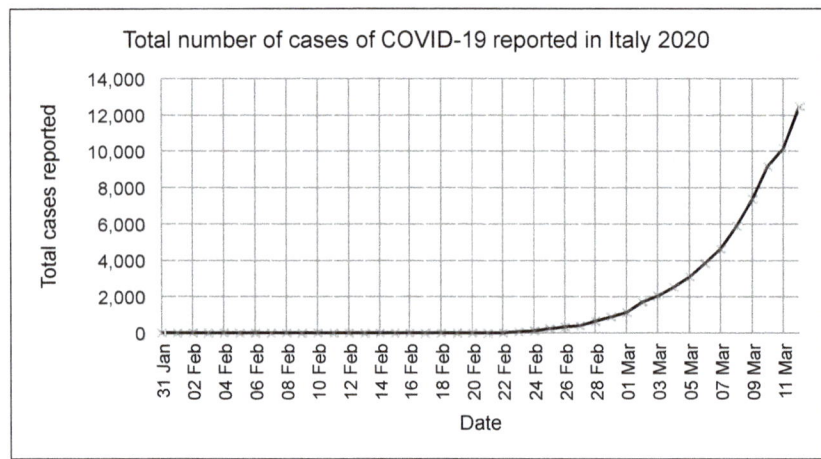

[Source: WHO. Data from 12 March 2020]

(d) State the number of cases in Italy on 3 March 2020 *and* 11 March 2020. [1]

(e) Calculate the percentage increase in the number of cases in Italy between 3 March and 11 March. [1]

....

The graph below shows the number of cases reported each day.

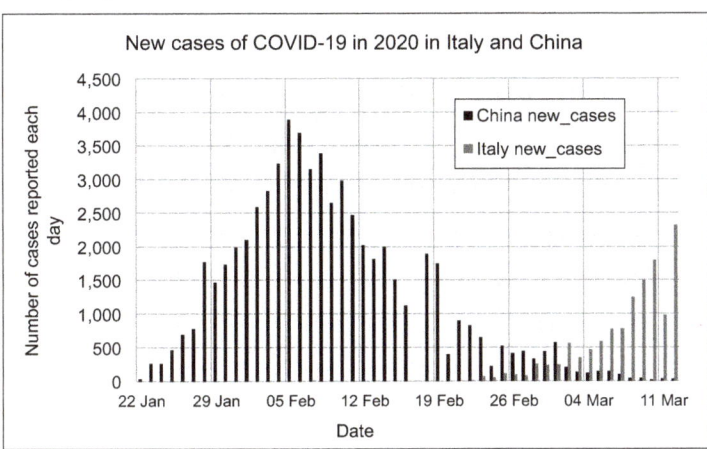

[Source: WHO, Data from 17 February 2020]

(f) Suggest one reason for the change in number of reported new cases in China after 5 February 2020. [1]

....

....

The table summarizes the epidemiological data from Italy and China on 5 February and 12 March 2020.

COVID-19	Country	Total cases	Total deaths	Percentage of deaths (%)
5 February 2020	China	24,363	491	2.0
	Italy	2	0	0
12 March 2020	China	80,981	3173	3.9
	Italy	12,462	827	6.6

[Source: WHO, https://www.who.int/docs/default-source/coronaviruse/20200312-sitrep-52-covid-19.pdf?sfvrsn=e2bfc9c0_2 https://www.who.int/docs/default-source/coronaviruse/situation-reports/20200205-sitrep-16-ncov.pdf?sfvrsn=23af287f_4]

(g) Suggest a reason why the death rate may not be accurate. [1]

....

....

(h) Based on all the data, compare and contrast the progress of the epidemic in the two countries. [3]

....

....

....

....

(i) The genome of the coronavirus COVID-19 was published on a global database by the Shanghai Public Health Clinical Center & School of Public Health on Gen bank.

State an advantage of publishing the genome on a global database. [1]

....

....

(j) Suggest a possible preventive measure for COVID-19. [1]

....

....

2. (a) The image shows a cell undergoing meiosis. Identify the stage of meiosis it is undergoing. [1]

....

(b) Explain how meiosis can result in Down syndrome. [2]

....

....

....

....

3. (a) Label the parts of the triglyceride diagram shown by I and II. [1]

I ....

II ....

(b) Describe how the covalent bonds are formed between the monomers in the triglyceride. [2]

....

....

....

....

(c) Compare the structure of a saturated and unsaturated fatty acid.
[1]

(d) Distinguish between a triglyceride and a phospholipid. [1]

Increased dietary intake of fats has been positively correlated with coronary heart disease which can lead to heart attacks.

(e) State the name of the artery that supplies the heart muscle with blood. [1]

(f) In coronary heart disease (CHD) a cholesterol plaque in the artery that supplies the heart could burst resulting in a blood clot forming at the site of the rupture.

Outline the process of blood clotting. [3]

4. The light micrograph below is of a *Helianthus*.

(a) Determine the organ this is from. [1]

(b) Identify tissue X and tissue Y and state what each tissue transports. **[2]**

....

....

(c) State one difference between the structure of the two tissues. **[1]**

....

....

(d) State the type of bond that occurs between water molecules. **[1]**

....

(e) Outline the importance of cohesion and adhesion in transpiration. **[3]**

....

....

....

....

....

NOTES

Section B

Answer **one question** from a choice of two. Up to one additional mark is available for the construction of your answers for each question.

5. Bacterial infections such as pneumonia can disrupt gas exchange in the lungs.

    (a) Compare and contrast the structure of a bacterial cell with a white blood cell. **[3]**

    (b) Outline the mechanism of ventilation. **[7]**

NOTES

(c) Describe how antibiotic-resistant bacteria give evidence for evolution. [5]

6. Autotrophs synthesize glucose and heterotrophs consume glucose. The glucose is then used in metabolism or stored in storage organs.

(a) Compare and contrast the structure of amylose and amylopectin. [4]

(b) Explain how blood glucose levels are controlled within narrow limits. [7]

NOTES

(c) Outline how energy flows in an ecosystem. **[4]**

Answers

Set A
Set A: Paper 1A

Question no.	Answer	Question no.	Answer	Question no.	Answer
1	D	15	D	29	D
2	C	16	C	30	C
3	C	17	A		
4	C	18	A		
5	D	19	B		
6	B	20	D		
7	D	21	B		
8	D	22	D		
9	A	23	C		
10	D	24	A		
11	B	25	C		
12	B	26	B		
13	D	27	B		
14	C	28	D		

Set A: Paper 1B

1. (a) Concentration of lactose/concentration of lactase **[1]**
   (b) (i) • Both have the optimum pH of 7
   • Both have similar/same relative enzyme activity at pH 6.5 and 7
   • Immobilized lactase has a significantly higher enzyme activity at pH 5.5–6
   • Immobilized lactase has a significantly higher enzyme activity at pH 7.5 and above **[Max 2]**
   (ii) • The lactase can be reused
   • Greater thermal and pH stability so less enzymes are denatured
   • Easy to purify the product/separate the enzyme from the product **[Max 1]**
   (c) • the graph shows the optimum pH to be near pH 7;
   • choose smaller range of pH (between 6.5 and 7.5);
   • smaller increments of pH.
   Accept numbers such as 0.5 or 0.1 **[2]**
   (d) • the research question identifies the independent variables (*effect of temperature/effect of immobilization*)
   • the research question identifies the dependent variable/derived value (*relative activity of lactase*) **[2]**

2. (a) Exercise amount, exercise and rest **[1]**
   (b) • At rest – 11 breaths in 55 seconds = (11/55) × 60 = 12 breaths per minute
   • During exercise – 11 breaths in 100 - 55 = 45 seconds So 11/45 × 60 = 14.6 breaths a minute (*accept 14 or 15*) **[1]**
   (c) • At rest – (0.6+0.6+0.6+0.6)/4 = 0.6 dm³
   • During exercise – (1.6+1.5+1.6+1.4)/4 = 1.55 dm³
   Accept answers from 1.5-1.6 **[2]**
   (d) • More oxygen is used in aerobic/cell respiration
   • The tidal volume and breathing rate increase **[Max 1]**
   (e) The ERV reduces because more air is forced out of the lungs when exhaling during exercise. **[1]**

3. (a) Rate of calcification of coral mmol $CaCO_3$ $m^{-2}h^{-1}$ **[1]**
   (b) • Light
   • Water depth
   • pH
   • Salinity
   • (Water) clarity
   • Temperature **[Max 1]**
   (c) • The higher seawater partial pressure/789 μatmr has significantly lower calcification rates
   • The higher seawater partial pressure/789 μatmr has lower calcification rates as the error bars don't overlap **[Max 1]**
   (d) • Easier to manipulate variables
   • Removes impact of other organisms
   • Small scale so many replicates can be carried out **[Max 1]**
   (e) • Other interactions in the actual environment/predation/competition may affect the results
   • Small-scale models are not always effective at predicting **[Max 1]**
   (f) • Increase in coral bleaching due to expulsion of Zooxanthellae
   • Loss of habitat for marine life/fish
   • Loss of marine biodiversity/more algae grow on dead coral
   • Mutualistic relationships with Zooxanthellae would be disturbed
   • Feeling/spawning sites for fish is lost/fish population fails **[1]**

4. (a) Scale bar is 20 mm = 20 000 μm
   Actual size of scale bar is 0.2 μm
   Magnification = image size/actual size
   Magnification = 20 000/0.2
   Magnification = x 10 000 **[1]**
   (b) Transmission electron microscope as it has a high magnification/high resolution/to see internal detail. **[1]**
   (c) Protein synthesis/synthesis of enzymes for photosynthesis **[1]**
   (d) Cryogenic Electron Microscopy/(Cryo-EM) **[1]**
   (e) Enzymes/substrates can be more concentrated; Substances that could cause damage to the cell can be kept inside the membrane of an organelle; pH can be maintained at an ideal level for a particular process (which may be different from the levels needed for other processes in a cell.); Organelles (with their contents) can be moved around within the cell; There is a larger area of membrane available (for processes that happen within or across membranes) **[1]**

Set A: Paper 2
Section A

1. (a) Eukaryota **[1]**
   (b) Antibiotics **[1]**
   (c) May 2005 **[Both month and year needed for 1]**
   (d) (i) (4 ÷ 27) × 100 = 14.8% **[1]**
   (ii) (1 ÷ 31) × 100 = 3.23% **[1]**
   (e) Similarities:
   • No TB found in either group Jan 05–Mar 05/or in first two months
   • Both had increases in TB near the end of the study
   • Both had no cases of TB in winter/(Jan–Mar)
   • Both had more possums not infected than infected
   Differences:
   • The first cases of TB are apparent in May 2005 in the control group, whereas TB is found in the vaccinated group in September 2005
   • Higher number of cases of TB are found in the control group and it is the converse for the vaccinated group **[Max 2]**
   (f) 600 pg/ml **[1]**
   (g) • Antibodies are higher in the vaccinated calves (peak 1250 pg/ml) compared to non-vaccinated (peak 600 pg/ml)
   • It is 106 weeks before antibody levels match the non-vaccinated calves/vaccine lasts long enough for practical reapplication **[2]**
   (h) • Effective as fewer possums that were vaccinated were infected by TB so less likely to pass it on to cows.
   • Effective in vaccinated calves as more interferon gamma/antibody is made
   • Effective as the antibody/interferon gamma is made faster
   • Not effective as offers short-term immunity/in both the non-vaccinated and BCG vaccinated the immune response/antibody production/IFN-γ drops significantly by 25 weeks
   • Not effective as no significant difference between non-vaccinated/control and vaccinated at 50+ weeks **[Max 3]**

2. (a) I – ovary
   II – stigma
   III – anther **[All three correct for 2 marks]**
   (b) • Insect-pollinated as colourful petals to attract insects
   • Insect-pollinated as pollen on anthers inside flower so will brush onto insects (as they make way to nectary)
   • Insect-pollinated as stigma inside flower so will brush onto insects (as they make way to nectary) **[Max 2]**

86

(c)
- The first name represents the genus and the second the species
- Unique combination of two names designates species worldwide/internationally
- They belong to the same genus/genus *Hyacinthoides*
- They are different species **[Max 2]**

3. (a) Polysaccharide **[1]**
   (b) Glycosidic **[1]**
   (c)
   - Amylopectin is made up of α-glucose whereas cellulose is made up of β-glucose
   - All glucose monomers are in same orientation in amylopectin but in cellulose the glucose alternates its orientation
   - Cellulose contains only 1,4 glycosidic bonds but amylopectin contains both 1,4 and 1,6 glycosidic bonds
   - Amylopectin is branched but cellulose is not/cellulose is straight chain
   - Cellulose contains hydrogen bonds between microfibrils **[Max 3]**
   (d) Amylopectin
   - Insoluble so doesn't affect osmosis/water potential so good storage molecule
   - Long molecule made up of many glucose monomers to provide energy
   - Branched so easily hydrolysed into glucose

   Cellulose
   - Hydrogen bonds between long straight chains in cell wall
   - Forms microfibrils/long and thin
   - Provides strength/rigidity/support **[Max 2]**

4. (a) G = 21%, C = 21%, T = 29% **[All correct for 1 mark]**
   (b)
   - They have different genes
   - Bases are in a different order
   - Different base sequences
   - So different amino acids/primary structure of proteins/polypeptides **[Max 2]**
   (c)
   - Single-stranded DNA
   - DNA as it contains T not U
   - Single-stranded as A isn't the same percent as T/C isn't the same percent as G
   - No complementary base pairing **[Max 2]**

5. (a) Sex: Female
   Reason: Two X chromosomes/Sex chromosomes are the same size/homologous/males would have an X and a Y/males would have different-sized sex chromosomes **[1]**
   (b) Metaphase of mitosis **[1]**
   (c) Non-disjunction **[1]**

Section B

6. (a) Diagram could include:
   - Phosphate
   - Deoxyribose sugar
   - Nitrogenous base/adenine, thymine, cytosine, guanine

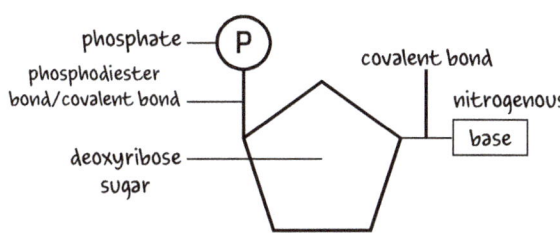

DNA nucleotide

[Max 3]

   (b)
   - RNA polymerase unwinds DNA strands/DNA strands are separated
   - RNA polymerase adds new nucleotides to template strand
   - by complementary base pairing/adenine (A) on the DNA template strand with uracil (U) on the mRNA strand
   - mRNA detaches from template strand/DNA strands rewind **[Max 4]**
   (c)
   - Caused by a mutation in the haemoglobin gene
   - Mutation results in a single base substitution (GAG → GTG) in the DNA sequence
   - Valine replaces glutamic acid (in the beta-globin protein)
   - Codominant inheritance / Normal allele is Hb_A **and** mutated allele is Hb_S
   - (Mutated allele) leads to misshaped red blood cells which can block blood flow, cause pain, and reduce oxygen transport.
   - Homozygous individuals ($Hb_S Hb_S$) have sickle cell disease
   - Heterozygous individuals ($Hb_A Hb_S$) are carriers / have sickle cell trait
   - Heterozygous individuals show symptoms under extreme conditions/ low oxygen levels.
   - Heterozygous advantage – carriers are more resistant to malaria/ Hb_S allele is more common in regions with high malaria prevalence.
   - 25% /0.25 chance that offspring of heterozygote parents have child with sickle cell anemia/$Hb_S Hb_S$ S)
   GENETIC SCREENING
   - DNA sequencing/ PCR detects the Hb_S mutation in the Hb gene.
   - Genetic screening of embryos for the mutation before implantation in in vitro fertilization (IVF).
   - Early diagnosis allows for better medical management
   [Max 8, 7 if no mention of genetic screening]

7. (a)
   - Carbon dioxide
   - Urea
   - Hormones
   - Antibodies/immunoglobulins
   - Urea
   - Water
   - Glucose/amino acid **[Max 3]**
   (b)
   - Damaged tissue/platelets release clotting factors
   - Platelets form a clot over the damaged tissue
   - Clotting factors start a cascade of reactions
   - Thrombin catalyses the conversion of inactive/soluble fibrinogen into active/insoluble fibrin
   - Fibrin forms a mesh/network of fibres over the damaged area/wound/clot
   - Fibrin traps red blood cells and white blood cells, forming a scab
   - Blood clot prevents the entry of pathogens/acts as a physical barrier **[Max 5]**
   (c)
   - Inherited recessive sex-linked condition
   - Gene for hemophilia is on X chromosome
   - Results in lack of clotting factor VIII/blood doesn't clot
   - X^H = allele for normal blood clotting
   - X^h = hemophiliac allele
   - Y = male
   Only females can be carriers/females have two copies of the X chromosome so can mask faulty allele
   - More males are hemophiliac than females
   - Males have one copy of X chromosome so cannot mask faulty allele/Males only need one copy of the gene to have hemophilia
   - Males cannot pass on hemophilia gene to sons/males pass Y chromosomes to sons
   - Sons inherit hemophilia from mothers only

Phenotype	Genotype
Normal female	$X^H X^H$
Carrier female (normal phenotype)	$X^H X^h$
Hemophiliac female	$X^h X^h$
Normal male	$X^H Y$
Hemophiliac male	$X^h Y$

- Example of a cross identifying parent phenotypes, genotypes and offspring e.g. carrier female ($X^H X^h$) × normal male ($X^H Y$) results in 1 normal female ($X^H X^H$) : 1 carrier female ($X^H X^h$), 1 hemophiliac male ($X^h Y$) : 1 normal male ($X^H Y$). Punnett grid or other valid example can be used:

Parent genotype	$X^H X^h$		
	Gametes	X^H	X^h
$X^H Y$	X^H	$X^H X^H$	$X^H X^h$
	Y	$X^H Y$	$X^h Y$

[Max 7]

Set B

Set B: Paper 1A

Question no.	Answer	Question no.	Answer	Question no.	Answer
1	C	15	A	29	B
2	D	16	B	30	B
3	D	17	C		
4	B	18	B		
5	D	19	A		
6	C	20	A		
7	A	21	C		
8	C	22	B		
9	D	23	D		
10	B	24	D		
11	D	25	D		
12	C	26	D		
13	A	27	C		
14	B	28	A		

Set B: Paper 1B

1. (a) • Surface area/size of cube
   • Time soaked for
   • Temperature **[Max 1]**
   (b) Potato – 0.32 mol dm^{-3} and sweet potato – 0.47 mol dm^{-3} **[2]**
   (c) Any value above 0.32 and below 0.47 **[1]**
   (d) • No repeats for each interval
   • Temperature not controlled
   • Potato/sweet potato not blotted to remove excess water **[2]**
   (e) Sweet potatoes contain significantly/lots more sugar per 100 g so they have a higher isotonic point **[1]**

2. (a) • Gauze to protect them from corrosive potassium hydroxide solution
   • Temperature range must not put organism under any stress
   • Only a few maggots to prevent overcrowding **[Max 1]**
   (b) • Allowed the respiration rate of the maggots to become constant
   • Allowed the maggots to reach the correct temperature
   • Allowed the gas inside the boiling tube to expand before the readings were recorded **[Max 1]**
   (c) • Answer 6/6.3/6.28 mm^3/min
   • Diameter of capillary tube $\pi r^2 = \pi \times 0.25 = 0.7854$ mm^2.
   • Volume bubble travelled in 5 minutes = $\pi r^2 \times$ length = 0.7854 mm^2 × 40 mm = 31.416
   • Rate of respiration per minute = 31.416/5 = 6.28 mm^3 per minute **[1]**
   (d) • As temperature increases the rate of aerobic respiration increases
   • Positive correlation between temperature and rate of respiration **[Max 1]**
   (e) • The maggots respire using up oxygen and the carbon dioxide produced is absorbed by the potassium hydroxide
   • The pressure inside the respirometer/boiling tube decreases causing the bubble to move to the left **[2]**
   (f) • A wider range of temperatures
   • Smaller intervals between the temperatures
   • A control containing the same mass of a non-living material/ glass beads **[Max 1]**

3. (a) • Scale bar image size with ruler = 12 mm = 12 000 μm.
   • Scale bar actual size = 5 μm
   • Magnification = image size / actual size = 12000/5 = × 2400
   • Stomatal pore measured diameter = 25 mm = 25,000 μm
   • Magnification = × 2400
   • Actual size = image size/magnification = 25000/2400 = 10.4 μm
   [Accept 10.3–10.5 μm] [1]
   (b) • When open, allows carbon dioxide and oxygen to diffuse through
   • When closed, prevents water loss /prevents transpiration **[2]**

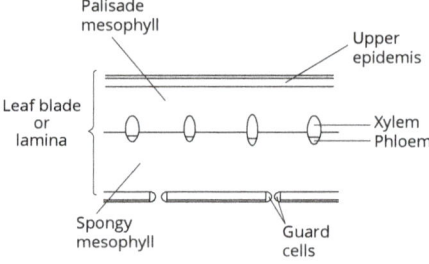

   (c) • upper epidermis
   • palisade mesophyll;
   • spongy mesophyll;
   • lower epidermis;
   • xylem/phloem/vascular bundle;
   1 mark for each correctly labelled tissue shown as a layer in proportion **[3]**

4. (a) 5 m: 19 and 10 m: 24 **[both needed for 2]**
   (b) • Species richness is related to number of different species in an ecosystem/A large number of different species in a habitat represents a higher species richness
   • Species evenness refers to the relative abundance/number of species types **[2]**
   (c) 14.7. OR 14.72 **[1]**

Set B: Paper 2

Section A

1. (a) 1988/1989/1990 **[1]**
   (b) Needs to be accurately measured: e.g.
   1958 = 315/6 and 2018 = 410/412
   412 – 316 = 96
   96 ÷ 316 ×100 = 30% **[1]**
   (c) • As atmospheric CO_2 increases, the seawater pCO_2 increases/ positive correlation between the atmospheric CO_2 and the seawater pCO_2
   • As atmospheric CO_2 increases, the pH decreases/negative correlation between the atmospheric CO_2 and the seawater pH
   • Correlation is not causation/other factors could be affecting the pH and ocean CO_2 **[Max 2]**
   (d) • Release of carbon dioxide into the atmosphere during combustion of coal/oil/natural gas/peat.
   • Deforestation has decreased uptake of carbon dioxide into forests.
   • Deforestation has increased release of carbon dioxide by respiring decomposers.
   • Destruction of peat bogs increases.
   • More carbon dioxide in atmosphere dissolves into oceans.
   [Max 3]
   (e) Eukaryota **[1]**
   (f) • As temperature increases mortality increases/there is a positive correlation between temperature and mortality
   • Greater increases between 3°C and 5.5°C than 5.5°C and 8°C
   • Differences are significant as error bars don't overlap **[Max 2]**
   (g) • Carbonic acid/H_2CO_3 dissociates/ionises
   • Forming H^+/hydrogen ions
   • H^+/hydrogen ions react with the CO_3^{2-}/carbonate ions
   • Less free CO_3^{2-}/carbonate ions in the ocean to build shells
   • Existing shells react with acid/H^+ ions
   • Shells dissolve/thin **[Max 3]**
   (h) • carbon dioxide will increase temperature/will reduce zooplankton/less food for salmon
   • Salmon population decreases
   • Economic impact (e.g. fishermen make less money) **[Max 2]**

2. (a) I – Phosphate
   II – Phosphodiester bond/sugar–phosphate bond
   III – <u>Deoxyribose</u> sugar
   IV – Base/nitrogenous base/guanine/adenine **[2]**
   (b) (i): Degenerate – more than one codon for each amino acid **[1]**
   (ii): Universal – the same DNA codes for the same amino acid in every species **[1]**
   (c) • Eukaryotes linear/prokaryotes circular
   • Prokaryotes have plasmids but eukaryotes do not
   • Eukaryotes associated with histone/proteins/prokaryotes have naked DNA/not associated with histone proteins
   • Eukaryotic DNA can supercoil but prokaryotic DNA cannot
   • Eukaryotes have more than one chromosome, prokaryotes have one **[Max 2]**
   (d) • DNA helicase: unzips/breaks the hydrogen bonds/separates

DNA strands
- DNA polymerase: joins sugar–phosphate backbone/forms phosphodiester covalent bond between nucleotides

Accept any of the following from HL material:
- DNA primase adds primers to the lagging strand
- DNA polymerase III adds nucleotides in a 5 carbon to 3 carbon direction/joins the sugar–phosphate backbone/phosphodiester bond/covalent bonds between sugars of one nucleotide and phosphate of another
- DNA Polymerase I/removes the primers
- DNA ligase joins the Okazaki fragments **[2]**

3. (a) Transmission electron microscope as virus is too small to be seen with a light microscope/higher resolution and magnification than light microscope. **[1]**

(b)
- Viruses are not made up of cells
- Viruses do not grow
- Viruses do not replicate
- They cannot perform (independent) metabolism
- They do not show characteristics of life (without a host) **[Max 2]**

(c)
- Antibiotics inhibit metabolic pathways/metabolism in prokaryotic cells
- Viruses don't have their own metabolic pathways/metabolism/Viruses use the host cells' metabolic pathways/metabolism
- Antibiotics do not inhibit/block host cell metabolism **[Max 2]**

4. (a)
- X is an artery.
- It has a thicker wall in relation to the lumen.
- It has a thicker muscular wall.
- It has a narrower lumen than veins.
- It has more elastic fibres than veins. **[Max 2]**

(b)
- Narrow lumen allows maintaining high pressure.
- Elastic tissue (in the walls) allows elastic recoil/maintain high blood pressure.
- Thick muscular tissue to withstand high pressure. **[Max 2]**

(c)
- feeling the carotid (neck) pulse with fingertips
- feeling the radial (wrist) pulse with fingertips
- Two/three fingertips are pressed (lightly) against the skin where the artery is located
- Using digital meters/pulse oximeters/smart watch **[Max 2]**
Accept other suitable digital meters.

Section B

5. (a)
- water (vapor) lost by transpiration/through stomata;
- transpiration/loss of water from leaves causes tension/transport of water in xylem;

Temperature:
- faster/more water loss/transpiration/transport in hotter weather;
- more heat energy/kinetic energy for evaporation from stomata;

Humidity:
- slower/less water loss/transpiration/transport in more humid weather due to a decreased concentration gradient/faster diffusion of water (vapor) out of the leaf/through the stomata with low humidity outside;

OR
no evaporation if air is saturated with water vapor/with 100% humidity;

Wind:
- faster/more water loss/transpiration/transport in windy/windier weather;
- wind/air movement carries away water vapor from around the leaf/stomata/increases concentration gradient;
- high winds can cause stomatal closure and so reduce transpiration;

Drought:
- drought causes stomata to close so reduces loss/transport; **[Max 5]**

(b)

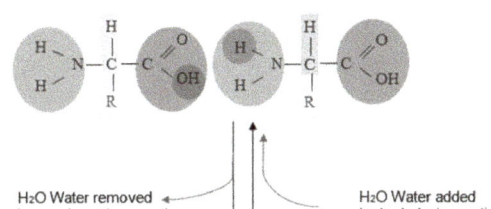

- Two correct amino acid structures drawn
- Molecule of water is released/condensation reaction between
- Correct dipeptide structure
- Peptide bond forms between the hydroxyl/OH from the carboxyl/COOH group is removed along with the H from the amino/NH₂ group of another amino acid **[Max 3]**

(c)
- Water is a polar molecule/the oxygen of one water molecule forms hydrogen bonds with the hydrogen of another
- Water is dense providing buoyancy, reducing the need for structural support in aquatic animals/making it easier to float.
- Black throated loon/*Gavia arctica* reduces buoyancy when diving by reducing lung air volume/bones not hollow so can dive underwater.
- Ringed seal/*Pusa hispida*: bones dense to allow diving/blubber less dense to allow floating.
- Water's higher viscosity compared to air increases resistance, requiring streamlined body shapes in aquatic animals.
- Black-throated loons/ringed seals have streamlined forms to reduce drag when in water.
- Viscosity of air is lower than water so loon can easily fly through air without expending much energy.
- Loons legs are towards rear of body to swim more effectively in viscous water/seal has flippers to push through viscous water.
- Thermal conductivity – water has a high specific heat capacity so it maintains a stable temperature/habitat.
- Loons feathers trap a layer of insulating air to reduce heat loss/Ringed seal has thick layer of waterproof fur that traps insulating air/thick layer of blubber to reduce heat loss.
- Water has a higher thermal conductivity than air so animals in water lose more heat than in air.
- Water has a high specific heat capacity/It takes a lot of heat energy to raise the temperature of water leading to a stable environmental temperature.
- Ringed seals do not have effective cooling mechanisms in air.
- Density of ice is less than water so forms an insulating layer/ice has lower thermal conductivity than water/providing habitat/stable temperatures. **[Max 7]**

6. (a)
- antigens stimulate antibody production;
- antibodies produced by lymphocytes;
- macrophages/phagocytes ingest/engulf pathogens and display antigens from them;
- T-cells activated by binding antigen/by macrophage displaying antigen;
- activated T-cells cause activation of B-cells;
- mitosis/division of (activated) B-cells (to produce a clone of cells)
- plasma cells formed from divided/activated/growing/differentiating B-cells;
- plasma cells/plasma B-cells secrete antibodies;
- clonal selection/plasma cells make same type of antibody/antibody specific to same antigen;
- some activated B-cells become memory cells; **[Max 5]**

(b)
- Circadian rhythm controls sleep/awake cycles
- Produced by the pineal gland;
- Acts on the hypothalamus
- Increased levels bring about sleepiness (in evening)
- decreased levels encourage waking (in morning)
- SCN cells detect light;
- Light decreases melatonin production **[Max 3]**

(c) Supporting evidence
- Evidence provides information about how humans and chimps may have diverged from their common ancestor.
- Humans have 46 chromosomes but chimpanzees have 48 (due to fusion of 12 and 13)
- Karyograms provide evidence for hypothesis as chimp chromosome 12 and 13 added together similar in length to chromosome 2
- No genes from the ends of primate/chimpanzee chromosomes 2A and 2B appear to have been lost;
- The banding pattern and DNA sequence of chromosome 2 in humans closely align with chromosomes 12 and 13 in chimpanzees.
- Human chromosome 2 has telomeres (normally found at chromosome ends) in the middle of human chromosome supports the idea of fusion, as telomeric sequences represent remnants of the chromosome ends that fused.
- Centromere in chimp chromosome 12 matches that of human chromosome 2
- Chromosome 2 has satellite/noncoding DNA/vestigial centromere where centromere of chimp chromosome 13 is located
- Supports fusion as ancestral chromosomes would each have had their own centromere, one of which became inactivated.

[Counterarguments or Limitations (2 marks)]
- The length of chimpanzee chromosomes 12 and 13 combined is not exactly the same as the length of human chromosome 2 (there is overlap). **[Max 7]**

Set C

Set C: Paper 1A

Question no.	Answer	Question no.	Answer	Question no.	Answer
1	C	15	B	29	B
2	D	16	B	30	B
3	B	17	C		
4	D	18	C		
5	B	19	D		
6	A	20	C		
7	B	21	C		
8	B	22	B		
9	B	23	B		
10	A	24	C		
11	B	25	B		
12	C	26	C		
13	B	27	A		
14	C	28	C		

Set C: Paper 1B

1. (a) Groups of organisms that can potentially interbreed to produce fertile offspring **[1]**

(b)
- Light (under canopy there is less light for photosynthesis)
- Availability of minerals/inorganic nutrients
- Space **[Max 1]**

(c)
- Random sampling
- Tape measure at right angles and randomly generating coordinates
- Place quadrat at co-ordinates **[2]**

(d)
- Use chi-squared test/X^2 test (for association)
- Equation must be written out $x^2 = \dfrac{\sum (O - E)^2}{E}$
- Correct expected values:

	Bluebells present	Bluebells absent
Wild garlic present	27.73	19.27
Wild garlic absent	31.27	21.73

- E = (row total × column total)/grand total:

	Bluebells present	Bluebells absent	Row Totals
Wild garlic present	27.73	19.27	47
Wild garlic absent	31.27	21.73	53
Column totals	59	41	100

- $X^2 = 46.45$

Species	Observed frequency O	Expected frequency E	O–E	(O–E)²	(O–E)²/E
Bluebells only	48	31.27	16.73	279.8929	8.95
Wild garlic only	36	19.27	16.73	279.8929	14.52
Both species	11	27.73	-16.73	279.8929	10.09
Neither species	5	21.73	-16.73	279.8929	12.88

$X^2 = 46.45$

- Degrees of freedom = (rows–1) × (columns–1) = 1
- Critical value = 3.841
- Value of X^2/46.45 greater than critical value/3.841 so there is an association between the two species **[4]**

2. (a) X = anaphase **[1]**

(b)
- Scale bar image size = 18 mm = 18,000 µm
- Actual size = 10 µm
- Magnification = image size/actual size = 18,000/10 = ×1,800
- Answer = ×1,800 **[1]**

(c) Measured length of Y = 55 mm × 1,000 = 55,000 µm
55,000/1,800 = 30.6 µm (any answer between 30 and 32 µm) **[1]**

(d)
- Water enters the cell by osmosis
- Increasing the turgor pressure of the cells/increasing size of cells/increasing length of cell Y. **[2]**

3. (a)
- In each population an increase in cholesterol increases the risk of CHD mortality
- Positive correlation **[1]**

(b) Northern Europe **[1]**

(c)
- Southern Europe mediterranean has a lower CHD mortality risk than Southern Europe inland
- Both have serum cholesterol levels between 3.65 and 6.50/similar range of cholesterol
- Both show an increase in cholesterol increases death rate by CHD
- (below 6.5 mmol) The risk of dying from CHD is approximately double in inland compared with mediterranean **[Max 2]**

(d)
- Mediterranean diet has a higher proportion of fibre
- Mediterranean diet has a higher proportion of unsaturated fat
- Mediterranean diet has a lower LDL cholesterol/higher HDL cholesterol
- Mediterranean diet has a higher proportion of unsaturated fat/lower proportion of saturated/trans fats
- Oils such as olive oil and fish oils are high in healthy omega 3 fatty acids/lower in omega 6
- Southern Europe mediterranean populations have lower genetic predisposition to CHD.
- Southern Europe mediterranean populations have obesity levels.
- Southern Europe mediterranean populations exercise more.
- Southern Europe inland smoke more. Accept converse. **[Max 1]**

(e)
- Can be supported as there is a positive correlation between cholesterol and CHD/as cholesterol increases CHD deaths in middle age men increase
- Can not be supported as correlation does not imply causation
- Can not be supported as many other factors affect CHD/example of factor
- Can not be supported as study only looked at middle aged men so is not valid for females or other ages
- Only high (LDL) cholesterol results in fatty deposits/atheroma in arteries but high HDL cholesterol reduces CHD **[Max 2]**

4. (a) The presence of <u>three</u> X chromosomes **[1]**
    (b) Non-disjunction (during Anaphase I or Anaphase II) **[1]**
    (c) • Recessive autosomal condition
        • For a child to inherit PKU they need two mutated alleles/homozygous for PKU alleles
        • caused by mutation in enzyme PAH/phenylalanine hydroxylase/enzyme needed to convert phenylalanine to tyrosine
        • enzyme cannot break down amino acid phenylalanine (to tyrosine)/Phenylalanine builds up in blood/brain
        • damaging brain/nervous system
        • treated by low protein diet **[Max 3]**

Set C: Paper 2
Section A

1. (a) Zoonosis/zoonotic disease **[1]**
    (b) 0.91 **[1]**
    (c) • Highest percentage death rate is MERS-CoV (quantified)
        • MERS has about 3 times the death rate SARS and 37 times the death rate of CoV-19
        • Greatest number of countries affected is CoV-19 / CoV-19 approximately 8/9 times the number of affected countries
        • Most total number of deaths caused by CoV-19/Death rate is 800 times higher than MERS-CoV and 9000 times higher than SARS-CoV
        • Most severe pandemic is SARS-CoV as significantly more people affected globally/pandemic **[Max 3]**
    (d) 3 March 2020: 2,000   11 March 2020: 10,000 **[1]**
    (e) (10,000−2,000) ÷ 2,000 × 100 = 400% **[(1) allow ECF from (a)] [1]**
    (f) • Fewer new cases as people who had the disease have died or recovered
        • More people were immune to the virus
        • Improved education/better awareness/improved hygiene/precautions/hand washing
        • Better treatments in hospitals
        • More hospitals/treatment centres set up/more doctors/nurses/healthcare assistants
        • Use of antiviral drugs/new medicines
          [Do not accept antibiotics]
        • Better diagnosis leading to identification of infected and isolation
        • Less contact with animals that spread the disease to humans **[1]**
    (g) • Not all people who have CoV-19 have been diagnosed so the death rate could be lower/some people have very mild symptoms/only test those presenting symptoms
        • Not enough capacity to test everybody for an accurate picture
        • Not all infected people who will die have died by 12 March as it's an ongoing epidemic so the final death rate could be higher **[Max 1]**
    (h) • Start of epidemic came first in China/later in Italy
        • Peak of epidemic in China is earlier than in Italy/China epidemic peaked on 4 February whereas Italy is highest on 12 March/not yet peaked by 12 March
        • Decrease in new cases in China but no decrease in new cases in Italy/China shows epidemic slowing down whereas in Italy it is still increasing
        • Higher maximum number of cases in China/converse for Italy
        • The rate of increase of new cases is similar in both countries
        • The death rate in Italy is higher/nearly double than China on 12 March
        • Italy's death rate of 6.6% is higher than the global death rate of 3.7%/China's death rate of 3.6% is similar to the global death rate of 3.7%
        • Large fluctuations in both countries **[Max 3]**
    (i) • International cooperation allows sharing of knowledge/collaborative research
        • Increases the chance of developing a vaccine
        • Increases the chance of developing antiviral drugs
        • Allows monoclonal antibodies to be made for diagnosis
        • Enables comparison of viral DNA to pangolin DNA to determine which animal originally transmitted the disease to humans **[Max 1]**
    (j) • Wearing masks
        • Social distancing
        • Movement of air
        • Vaccination **[Max 1]**

2. (a) Anaphase II/two/2 **[1]**
    (b) • Non-disjunction
        • Failure of separation of homologous chromosomes/pairs of chromosomes (in anaphase I)
        • Failure of separation of sister chromatids (in anaphase II) **[Max 2]**

3. (a) I – Glycerol, II – Fatty acids **[All correct for 1 mark]**
    (b) • (Condensation reaction/loss of water)
        • Between the carboxyl/COOH group of fatty acid and the hydroxyl/OH group of glycerol
        • Or an image to show the above **[Max 2]**
    (c) A saturated fatty acid has single carbon to carbon/C–C bonds whereas an unsaturated fatty acid has a double carbon to carbon bond/C=C/between carbon atoms
        [Do not accept double bonds without reference to carbon atoms] **[1]**
    (d) • Triglyceride has three fatty acids, but phospholipid has two
        • Phospholipid has a phosphate group attached to the glycerol but the triglyceride does not
        • Phospholipids are amphipathic/have both hydrophobic and hydrophilic properties but triglycerides are hydrophobic **[Max 1]**
    (e) Coronary artery **[1]**
    (f) • Clotting factors are released
        • Platelets form a plug (at the rupture site)
        • Thrombin catalyses/converts fibrinogen to fibrin
        • Fibrin is insoluble and forms a mesh of fibres around the plug/fibrin traps blood cells forming a clot **[Max 3]**

4. (a) Stem **[1]**
    (b) X – phloem – transports sugar/sucrose/amino acids/organic compounds
        Y – xylem – transports water (and minerals) **[2]**
    (c) • Phloem has smaller diameter tubes/sieve plates/more cytoplasm in cell/companion cells
        • Xylem has a thicker wall
        • Xylem has a wider lumen
        • Xylem is lignified
        • Xylem cells are dead whereas phloem are living **[Max 1]**
    (d) Hydrogen **[1]**
    (e) • Water molecules are polar/dipoles (so form hydrogen bonds)
        • Cohesion is when water molecules form (hydrogen) bonds with other water molecules
        • Adhesion is when water molecules form (hydrogen) bonds with other surfaces
        • Cohesion transmits the tension/transpiration pull from the leaves to the stem to the roots/maintains a continuous column of water
        • Adhesion is when water is attracted to xylem stopping column breaking/replaces water that has evaporated by adhesion with (cellulose) cell walls **[Max 3]**

Section B

5. (a) • Bacteria cell has a nucleoid where as a white blood cell has a nucleus
        • Bacterial cell has plasmids where as white blood cells do not.
        • Bacterial cells have 70S ribosomes but white blood cells have 80S ribosomes
        • Bacterial cells have flagella but white blood cells do not
        • White blood cells have membrane bound organelles/mitochondria/lysosomes/rough ER where as bacterial cells do not.
        • Both have cell membrane and cytoplasm and DNA **[Max 3]**
    (b) • Ventilation consists of inhalation and exhalation
        Inhalation
        ○ External intercostal muscles contract and move up and out
        ○ The diaphragm contracts and moves down
        ○ The volume in the thorax increases...
        ○ ...reducing the pressure
        ○ This means the pressure is below atmospheric pressure
        ○ Air flows from the atmosphere into the lungs to equalize the pressure/from a high to low pressure
        Exhalation
        ○ Exhalation involves relaxing of external intercostal muscles or contraction of internal intercostal muscles
        ○ The diaphragm relaxes and moves up...
        ○ ...increasing pressure in thorax

- o Air flows from the lungs to the atmosphere to equalize the pressure/from a high to low pressure
- o Forced exhalation involves contraction of internal intercostal muscles **[Max 7]**

(c)
- Evolution is the change in heritable characteristics of a species over time
- Mutations occur in the DNA of bacteria
- Leading to variation in the resistance to antibiotics
- The introduction of antibiotics alters the environment/causes a selection pressure
- Bacteria not resistant to antibiotics are killed/the bacteria with the antibiotic-resistant mutation survive/survival of the fittest antibiotic-resistant bacteria
- The fittest reproduce (by binary fission)
- The population now all contain the antibiotic resistance **[Max 5]**

6. (a)
- Both are polymers of the monomer alpha/α glucose/both are hydrolysed into alpha/α glucose
- Both are polysaccharides used for storage in plants
- 70/80% of starch has amylopectin, and only 20/30% of starch has amylose in its structure
- Both contain 1, 4 glycosidic bonds
- Only amylopectin contains 1,6 glycosidic bonds
- Amylopectin is branched whereas amylose is linear/unbranched
- Amylose can be hydrolysed/release its energy more quickly than amylopectin (due to branching)
- Amylose is insoluble in water whereas amylose is soluble
- Amylose has 300,000 monomers of glucose whereas amylopectin has up to 200,000 units of glucose/amylose has more monomers of glucose

[Also accept diagrams for any of the points] [Max 4]

(b)
- High blood glucose levels are detected by the pancreas/islets of Langerhans
- Beta/β cells secrete the hormone insulin
- Insulin travels in the blood to target organs
- Insulin increases cellular respiration in cells
- Insulin increases the uptake of glucose into liver and muscle cells
- Liver and muscle cells convert soluble glucose to insoluble glycogen – which lowers blood glucose
- If blood glucose is too low the hormone glucagon is released
- Glucagon stimulates the conversion of glycogen to glucose
- Glucagon raises blood sugar
- Negative feedback mechanism **[Max 7]**

(c)
- energy from the sun is captured by plants/autotrophs;
- light energy is converted to chemical energy by photosynthesis;
- energy is passed to animals/consumers/along the food chain;
- at each stage in the food chain energy is lost by respiration/as heat;
- much less energy/only about 10% is available at each stage/trophic level of the food chain;
- (some) energy is made available to decomposers when organisms die/parts fall to the ground;
- energy is not recycled **[Max 4]**

www.ingramcontent.com/pod-product-compliance
Lightning Source LLC
Chambersburg PA
CBHW061055170426
43191CB00022B/2442